A Dictionary of Urglaawe Terminology

A Dictionary of Urglaawe Terminology

Robert L. Schreiwer
Distelfink Urglaawischi Sippschaft
Bristol, PA

Ammerili Eckhart
Hottenstein Urglaawischer Freibesitz
Schubert, PA

31. Hadding, 2012

Copyright © 2012, Robert L. Schreiwer, Ammerili Eckhart

All rights reserved. No part of this book may be reproduced, stored, or transmitted by any means—whether auditory, graphic, mechanical, or electronic—without written permission of both publisher and author, except in the case of brief excerpts used in critical articles and reviews. Unauthorized reproduction of any part of this work is illegal and is punishable by law.

ISBN 978-1-105-51712-9

About the Authors

Robert Lusch Schreiwer grew up in a traditional Deitsch (Pennsylvania German) setting. His education took him into Slavic Studies, including spending eighteen months in the erstwhile Yugoslavia in 1986-1987. Upon returning from Croatia, Rob earned his Bachelor of Arts degree in Eastern European Studies, including the Russian and Croatian languages. In 2005, he completed his Master of Arts degree in Slavic Studies, again including the Russian and Croatian languages.

In 2008-2009, Rob served as the Instructor of Pennsylvania German at Kutztown University. Through his time teaching his native language in the university setting, he discovered that he enjoyed teaching. He returned to college and earned his Elementary Education certification from Temple University in 2011 and his Special Education certification in 2012.

The many living traditions in Deitsch culture led Rob in 2007 to organize the Old Ways into a Heathen path called Urglaawe, which means "primal faith" in the Deitsch language. In 2008, Rob and Deborah Wheeler founded Die Urglaawisch Sippschaft vum Distelfink (commonly called Distelfink Sippschaft), which was the first Urglaawe kindred to be formed. As of the date of this writing, Distelfink Sippschaft has over 20 members and associates. Rob still serves as Ziewer, or godsman, of the kindred.

Braucherei is the Elder tradition of healing that has thrived in the Deitscherei (Pennsylvania German or Pennsylvania Dutch Country) since the Colonial Era, but its roots run deep into Continental German pre-Christian history and include the awareness of the Teutonic deities. Rob had always been familiar with Braucherei, having visited the folk or shamanic doctors alongside medical doctors since childhood.

In 2008, Rob completed the *Braucherei Weg* course at the Three Sisters Center for the Healing Arts. He then entered the apprenticeship, under mentor Jesse Tobin, with the Oley Freindschaft Raad, which is the oldest Braucherei lineage in North America. He is now a Braucher and practices the Old Ways in an Urglaawe context. He also maintains the Lüsch-Müsselman Graabhof - Urglaawe cemetery in Carbon County, PA.

In 2011, Rob was elected to serve on the High Rede (council) of The Troth, which is a national Heathen organization.

Also in 2011, Rob was part of a core group of parents and educators who founded the Deitschi Vorschul (Pennsylvania German Preschool) in Berks County, PA. This preschool is a summer camp that imbues the children with traditional Deitsch cultural sensitivities and concepts, including an understanding of Braucherei, stewardship of the land, and, of course, the Deitsch language.

Rob continues to be highly active in the advancement of the Deitsch language and culture. He writes and maintains several prominent Deitsch websites and blogs, and he is a regular contributor to Deitsch-oriented journals and radio broadcasts.

Ammerili Eckhart grew up in a conservative Mennonite setting. Although Mennonite groups expressly forbid the incorporation of Heathen practices in the lives of their members, old traditions do not disappear easily. Ammerili learned elements of Braucherei in the form of "laying on the hands," but her mentor taught her some of the aspects of the practice that originated in pre-Christian times.

Ammerili entered the apprenticeship of the Parryville-Harrity Braucherei Freindschaft in 2004 and received the power in 2006. Since that time, Ammerili has trained two Brauchers from their apprenticeship to their mastery.

In 2010, after conducting some research into Urglaawe rites, Ammerili formed the Hottenstein Urglaawischer Freibesitz, which is commonly known as Hottenstein Freibesitz. She currently serves as the Ziewerin, or priestess/godswoman of the fellowship.

Ammerili practices Braucherei in an Urglaawe context in Berks, Lehigh, and Schuylkill Counties, PA.

About Urglaawe

The Teutonic peoples of Northern Europe once embraced their traditional folk religion, which had been a guiding force in their lives since time immemorial. Their religion was based on worshiping their deities, honoring their ancestors, building a community with their kin and their neighbors, and respecting the land and its spirits.

Beginning with the reign of Roman Emperor Constantine I (272-332), Christianity became the dominant religion in the Empire. As the European nations converted to Christianity, the adherents to the old ways suffered, often severely, if they refused to abandon their folk faith in favor of the new religion. The Church was harsh in its treatment of anything that smacked of the pagan faiths. The old religions and philosophies were nearly exterminated.

However, we are fortunate that the annihilation was not complete. The collision of the Christian world with the Teutonic world brought about a Germanization of Christianity (see Russell's *The Germanization of Early Medieval Christianity* for the definitive analysis of the process). Writings, traditions, oral lore, folklore, superstitions, and other aspects of the old faith have survived to the present day. Various traditions and practices lived on among different Teutonic tribes, including some of the tribes that eventually merged together to form the Pennsylvania German (Deitsch) nation.

In the pre-Christian days, our religion had no name; it was just a part of life that was engrained in the culture. Today, we know of different varieties of this religion by various names, including Ásatrú, Forn Sidu, Theodism, and others. "Heathenry" or "Heathenism" is an umbrella term for all the modern manifestations of the old religion. The specific term for the faith as seen through the lens of the Deitsch (Pennsylvania Dutch or Pennsylvania German) culture is Urglaawe.

"Urglaawe" means "primal faith" in Deitsch. As a tradition within Heathenism, it bears some affinity to Ásatrú and to the other traditions that have emerged from Germanic paganism. Robert L. Schreiwer and Patricia Niedrich coined the term in 2007 on Niedrich's Hexenkunst Yahoo Group. It should be stressed that, while the term Urglaawe is young, the traditions that Urglaawe draws upon are aspects of the living Deitsch culture and folkways. The practices and beliefs are old; the organizational structure is new.

Urglaawe derives its core primarily from the Deitsch language, from folklore, from customs, and also from the Elder healing practice of Braucherei, which was a widespread practice among the Deitsch people until well into the 20th century. Continental German and Scandinavian lore serve as secondary and tertiary sources, respectively.

As is the case with other Teutonic religions and philosophical traditions, adherents of Urglaawe may have differing beliefs that range from polytheistic reconstruction to syncretistic, pragmatic psychologist, or mystical approaches.

Despite the fact that the German regions of Europe were Christian for many centuries prior to the Diaspora to the Americas, quite a few Heathen practices continued among the Pennsylvania Germans after emigration from Europe. Some historical references belie the presence of Heathen practices among the Deitsch. For example:

> *"Not all Pennsylvania-German pioneers were good Christian people. With such as were not, sin did abound, and men were given to idolatry, giving to the creature what is to be given to God only; they abused God's name by profanity, by superstitious practices..."* - Schantz, J.F.J., 1900. "The Domestic Life and Characteristics of the Pennsylvania-German Pioneer" p 80. Lancaster, PA: The Pennsylvania German Society.

Another example of a reference the continuity of old traditions in the modern world:

> *"Religion has many levels. For those who believe in powwowing, it is just as much a part of their religion as anything they hear or say or sing in church. Anthropologists have coined the term "folk religion" for these primitive survivals in society. Powwowing is Pennsylvania's best example of the survival power of the "old religion" of medieval Europe in a New World and Protestant setting."* - Yoder, Don, 1966. *Twenty Questions on Powwowing.* "Pennsylvania Folklife" vol. 15, no 4, pp. 39-40.

The deities of Urglaawe are the same as those of Norse Mythology. However, the perceptions of individual deities may differ, and some deities may be more prominent in one Heathen path than in another. For example, one of the principal deities in Urglaawe is Holle. Additionally, some deities, such as Ewicher Yeeger, are known in Urglaawe but unknown in other Heathen sects. Urglaawe embraces the awareness from other Heathen sects of deities who were previously unknown in modern Deitsch culture (e.g., Idunn, Gefjon, etc.).

Urglaawe also has a component of ancestor veneration. The deities are viewed as elder kin. There are numerous entities, such wights, dwarves, and elves that are also venerated.

The organization of rites in Urglaawe is rooted mostly in Braucherei ceremonial structures. Perhaps fortuitously, Braucherei ceremonies are very similar in function and execution to the sumbles of other Heathen traditions. Thus, the Urglaawe Sammel would feel very familiar to adherents of the various sects of Heathenry.

Relationship to Braucherei

The guiding principles of Urglaawe and Braucherei are very similar. One key difference, though, is that Braucherei is considered to be a spiritual healing practice, not a religion. Urglaawe is a faith.

Individuals of a variety of religious backgrounds can practice Braucherei. The tradition has been exposed to many different influences over the centuries, and individual practitioners have varied in their adoption of these influences. There is no doubt that some of the features of Braucherei, particularly its ceremonies, originated in pre-Christian practice. These are the aspects of Braucherei that Urglaawer treasure the most. Also, Braucherei has passed along, mostly through a rich oral tradition, a significant amount of lore and wisdom from the remote past.

However, not all Brauchers know or utilize these traditions. Many Brauchers practice solely in a Christian context. Braucherei is a large and complex tradition, and for most Brauchers, the confluence of the traditions is acceptable. This is a key difference between Urglaawe and Braucherei: Urglaawe is a strictly Heathen path.

Thus, Braucherei and Urglaawe are related but very different. In some ways, they are wrapped around one another because Braucherei carries many unbroken pre-Christian practices. Urglaawe is a continuation of the pre-Christian faith as viewed through the lens of the Deitsch culture today.

Urglaawe is a religion, a philosophy, a spiritual construct, and a way of life.

Explanation of Entries

The entries in this book are arranged alphabetically by principle component.

Verbs are entered in their infinitive form in bold print, followed by their past participial forms in regular type. For example:

daafe, gedaaft

The bold entry, "daafe," indicates that it is the infinitive of the verb, meaning "to sprinkle with water." The "gedaaft" indicates that it is the past participle, meaning "sprinkled with water."

Nouns are entered in bold. Deitsch nouns are preceded by the definitive article reflecting their grammatical gender in the nominative case. The four nominative definitive articles are as follows:

<u>Singular</u>
der: masculine
die: feminine
es: neuter

<u>Plural</u>
die: for all genders

For example:

der **Urglaawe**

The main noun entry is "Urglaawe." The "der" article indicates that the noun is of the masculine grammatical gender.

Some noun entries include masculine, feminine, and/or plural forms.

die **Eed**; plural: die **Eede**

This entry indicates that the singular noun "Eed" is of the feminine grammatical gender. The plural of the noun is "Eede."

der **Diener** (male); die **Dienerin** or **Dienern** (female): Clergy.

This entry indicates that "Diener" is a noun referring to male clergy while "Dienerin" and "Dienern" are terms to refer to female clergy.

While it is not necessary for English speakers to memorize the article or the grammatical gender of a word, the information is provided in order to help those who use the Deitsch language in Urglaawe rituals to know how to utilize the terms correctly.

An entry that includes a word in *italics*, with the exception of a book titles, serves to direct the reader to other terms that relate to the entry. For example:

> der **Aadler**: Eagle. On the *Muunraad,* the...

The italicization of "Muunraad" indicates that there is an entry for that term, and the reader may wish to view it for more information.

A Dictionary of Urglaawe Terminology

der **Aadler**: Eagle. On the *Muunraad,* the tenth new moon after Oschdre (the spring equinox) is the eagle moon.

die **Aarufing**: Invocation. This is a long chant that takes place before outdoor ceremonies. It consists of a call to the wights of the four directions, of above, and of below. It also serves as a call to participants to come for the ceremony.

der **Abbel** (singular), die **Ebbel** (plural): Apple. Numerous Deitsch proverbs speak of the healing and sustaining power of apples. In a similar manner, Scandinavian lore provides the tale of the goddess Idunn and Her apples, which sustain the deities and prevent Them from aging.

die **Addning**: The Noble Virtue of Discipline. Self-control, moderation, and respect for oneself and for others are critical aspects of the concept of living life conscientiously and deliberately rather than simply existing on whim and reaction. See *Reenheide*.

es **Ael**: Ale. Ale is a beverage used in many Urglaawe rituals, particularly those honoring *Dunner*. See also *Drankopfer*.

die **Aernet**: The month of August.

die **Alcis** (plural noun): See *Alhiz*.

der **Aldaar**: Altar. Urglaawe altars are typically fairly elaborate. During ceremonies, a wide array of flower and herb offerings are usually presented to the deities. Statuary, steins (*Seidel*), incense, a ceremonial bowl (*Schissel*), and other votive offerings or decorative items may grace the altar.

Aldi Fraa, die **Alt Fraa**: "Old Lady," mugwort. This is perhaps the most frequently used smudging herb in the Deitsch culture. It is a vaunted herb sacred to Holle. It is one of the oldest incense herbs in Europe (Müller-Ebeling, Rätsch & Storl 10). Aldi Fraa is used to promote dreaming and as a bug repellent (Hess *Mugwort* 11).

Christopher Sauer, a Deitscher who wrote America's first book of botanical healing, described Aldi Fraa as one of the key herbs in Deitsch folk medicine (Weaver 218). He also used the German name "Beyfuss" (modern German spelling would be "Beifuß"), stating that the term refers to the "goosefoot" tracks made by witches who used the plant for numerous practices.

Sauer also states that the name "Aldi Fraa" is a reference to the "goose mother whose origins may trace to the consort of the Gaulish god of war" (Weaver 218). Despite the inclusion of a Celtic war god, Sauer draws a clear relationship between mugwort and *Holle* or *Berchta*, to both of whom references to geese are applicable.

die **Alhiz**: Plural noun. This is a reference to the Alcis, whom Tacitus describes as being worshiped by the Germanic Naharnavali (of Silesia, a region that contributed settlers who became part of the Deitsch nation) tribe. Tacitus compares the Alhiz to the Roman Castor and Pollux. Like Castor and Pollux, the Alhiz are twin gods. However, there is no reason to assume that they were worshiped as a result of foreign influence (Simek 7). In Urglaawe, these gods are seen as protective deities, particularly over boys and brothers, and the rune Elhaz is associated with their protection. Simek (7) postulates that they may have been horse gods, which lends some credence to theories identifying them as Hengist and Horsa, the brother gods from Anglo-Saxon lore.

es **Alleliewezel**: The 31st of Gehling, or October, also known as Halloween. Due to the thinness of the veil between the physical and spiritual planes (Boyer, *Soul* 2-3), this traditionally is a time that Brauchers aid Holle to seek out the souls of the recently departed. As Holle rises to lead the Wild Hunt (see *Wildi Yacht*), the soul workers guide the spirits to Her *Miehl*. This observance also begins the *Schlachtzeit*.

die **Allemaengel**: A region in Lynn Township, Lehigh County, and Albany Township, Berks County, which has long been a stronghold of sorcery (Smith 2). In particular, *Walpurgisnacht* is reputed to be a spiritually active time, which relates the area to *Holle* from an Urglaawe perspective. Legends of the *Hexdanz* emerge of from the area as early as the Palatine settlement (Yoder *A Legend,* 5).

Interestingly, this area includes areas in which Ewicher Yeeger has made His presence known. The area has a harsh Colonial history (Stine *Allemengel* 10) reflected in the meaning of its name "all deficiencies." Thus, there is some reason to accept claims that it was to this area Ewicher Yeeger drove the game that saved the settlers. See also *Hexekopp, Hexebaerrick.*

alu: Magical word that appears on runic inscriptions and bracteates. While the word means "ale," it bears the connotation of ecstasy or magic (Simek 11-12). The word is often spoken, alone or in combination with other words, over the stein (*Seidel*) as part of sanctifying the beverage for ceremonial consumption. The spoken word is typically accompanied by tracing the runic letters (Ansuz, Laguz, Uruz) over the libation.

die **Ase**: The tribe of deities known in Scandinavian lore as the Aesir. The Ase are considered to be deities of consciousness and higher thought. Among the most familiar of the Ase are *Ziu, Wodan, Frigg, Dunner,* Siwwa, Idunn, *Volla, Zisa,* and many others. See also *Wane*.

die **Ausdauer**: This is the Noble Virtue of Perseverance or Steadfastness, including plodding forth in the face of adversity or challenge. The ancillary virtue of *Weisheit* (Wisdom) can help us to know the difference between being steadfast and being obdurate.

Steadfastness for appropriate purposes is wise. Stubbornness and a denial of reality are foolish. See *Reenheide*.

die **Ausdeeling**: Distribution. At the end of the sole round of *Sege*, the remainder of the libation in the Stein (*Seidel*) or Horn is poured into a sacred *Schissel*. The libation is then distributed by way of a blessed twig (see *Segezweig*) onto the heads of the participants, whether by sprinkling or by the drawing of a rune.

der **Baer**: Bear. In some areas, a fox or a bear fulfilled the role of the groundhog (*Grundsau)* as prognosticator. In the areas where a bear took on that role, the weather was determined by whether the bear was able to see over the mountain. This may be the root of the old song, "The Bear Went Over the Mountain," which includes the line of "to see what he could see" (Yoder *Groundhog* 52-54).

On the *Muunraad*, the seventh new moon after Oschdre (the spring equinox) is the bear moon. It is uncertain whether the Muunraad's utilization of the bear, in the role of prognosticator, plays any part in the timing of the animal's moon. If so, a bear's early or late entry into hibernation may serve to predict the harshness of the coming winter.

See also *Grundsau, Fux*.

der **Balder**: Son of *Frigg* and *Wodan*. See also *Phol*.

der **Barrickschpitz**; plural: die **Barrickschpitze**: Mountaintop or peak. In Urglaawe, there are nine sacred mountaintops across the central portion of the Deitscherei. Some of the mountaintops are along the same ridge, particularly on the Blobarrick (Blue Mountain ridge). The nine sacred peaks are: Cushion Peak, Eagle's Peak, Hawk Mountain, The Pinnacle, Hexenkopf, Mount Penn, Yellow Mountain, Mount Pisgah, Blue Mountain Peak. Some of the peaks, such as Hexenkopf, Yellow Mountain, and Blue Mountain Peak, are associated with a particular deity or event.

der **Bann**: Banning charm. The term may refer either to a physical object, such as amulet or talisman, or to an incantation or a written charm. See also *Zauber, Zing*.

der **Banner** (male); die **Bannerin** (female); die **Banner** (plural): This is a general term for a magician who engages in banning or banishing objects or entities.

die **Bannerei**: Banning magic. This is a generic term for magic that involves banning. It takes on the connotations of neither Braucherei nor Hexerei. See also *Zauberei*.

der **Barick**: Barrow. A barrow used in the transporting of the body or memorial item during an Urglaawe funeral rite. The barrow is burned in the funeral pyre (*Leichtfeier*), regardless of whether the body is buried or cremated.

Barrow constructed by Patrick Donmoyer. Photo by Peter B. Schlegel.

es **Bedenk**: Scruple, ethic, thew. This is a general term for an ethical value.

die **Bedrachdung**: Meditation. Meditation in Urglaawe most typically involves the use of runes (see *Roon*). However, incantations and chants from Braucherei may be used to bring the practitioner into an altered, meditative state. See also *Entzicke*.

der **Belsnickel**, der **Belschnickel**: A byname for Wodan. See *Wodan, Yuul*.

die **Belsnickeling**: See *Yuul*.

die **Berchta**: Goddess most likely of the *Wane*. She is seen either as a sister to *Holle* or as Holle by another name. Her holiday is 31. Yuuling (see *Berchtaslaaf*). As is the case with many Teutonic goddesses, She is known for spinning. In the post-Heathen era, Her honor has been tainted by the Church, though the horrid masks that appear as depictions of the Wild Hunt (*Wildi Yacht*) in parts of Germany and Switzerland carry both a fear and a respect for the powerful goddess. See also *Aldi Fraa, Gans*.

der **Berchtaslaaf**: Progression of the goddess Berchta, December 31 (31. Yuuling). Celebration includes food of gruel and fish, which is Berchta's prescribed meal. Urglaawer typically make the fare to consist of herring and oatmeal or dumpling and herring meal (Grimm, *Teutonic* 273).

der **Blanzeschwetze**: Blanzeschwetze (literally "to talk to plants") is a form of traditional herbal wisdom that is commonly known among practitioners of Braucherei. It incorporates herbal lore (medical and occult), and it aids in the communication among living creatures for the purposes of healing (see *Zusaagpflicht*). Blanzeschwetze is an element in gardening (weeding, selection of plant locations, companion planting, etc.). It is both a practical folkway and an esoteric tradition.

die **Blobottel**: Cornflower (Centaurea cyanus). The significance of this flower has wide interpretations across the German-speaking lands. The meanings of many symbols, particularly those that relate to Prussia, are based in historical events that occur after the Migration. However, certain aspects of the flower, particularly those that preserve the color and overall essence of the flower when dried, make it a symbol of life. Likewise, the tenderness of the flower and its susceptibility to frost make it a symbol of the preciousness and fragility of life. The presence of Cornflower Queens or cornflowers at events such as the Steuben Parade (Philadelphia, PA: http://phila.steubenparade.com/de/cornflower.htm) is an echo and a reflection of the flower's symbol of life.

There is some speculation that the Blobottel may be the blue flower in the dreams of Yorinde in the folk tale of *Yorinde un Goringel* (a version of which appears in Barrick *German-American* 109). The possessor of the flower is able to destroy enemies and to overcome obstacles.

es **Blutvergiesse**: Bloodletting. A form of *Sege* involving live sacrifice. See also *Fagge*.

der **Braucher** (male); die **Braucherin** (female); die **Braucher** (plural): A practitioner of the Elder tradition of Braucherei, also called Powwow (possibly a loan word from Lenape but equally likely from the Deitsch pronunciation of the English word "power"). Additional connotations are "witch doctor," "folk doctor," "shaman," and "healer."

die **Braucherei**: Powwow. Yvonne Millspaw (14) describes Braucherei as "a form of healing based on ancient continental European magical and religious beliefs." Braucherei employs amulets, incantations, prayers, blessings, charms and conjurations in ritual (Millspaw 14, White 25). It is literally translated from the Pennsylvania Dutch as "trying," but it is often referred to by its English designation, "powwowing" (Millspaw 14).

Braucherei is an Elder tradition that has survived the ages in various Continental Germanic areas, but it is most clearly identified with the Deitsch culture. During the Migration era (1683-1820), people from numerous areas of what is now Germany came to Pennsylvania and adjacent areas. While some waves of these migrants were hardcore Christians, the bulk of them were economic immigrants who were fleeing the shattered economy of the German lands. These people brought many old traditions with them. (Milnes 5-10). Braucherei was among them.

This healing practice was a dominant force in Deitsch communities up until the Pennsylvania government began attempts to suppress the Deitsch culture beginning in the World War I era (Tobin *Weg*, month 3). Laws regulating the practice of medicine (some written to target Braucherei) also were written, thus driving much of the practice underground by 1920 (White 26-27).

While most Braucherei practitioners would have considered themselves Christians, many followed folk religions, syncretistic beliefs, or Heathen "old ways," whence Urglaawe is able to find ancient traditions in the living Deitsch culture. Influences from

Braucherei traveled down the Appalachian range and into the Piedmont (Montgomery *American* 52-53) and impacted diverse practices, such as Hoodoo (Milnes 15-17).

See also *Hexerei, Meege, Wille*

die **Brechthelft**: The Bright Half (or Light Half) of the year begins on Moifescht (see *Wonnetdanz*). The physical realm is governed by Wodan at this time. This is a time of spiritual illumination and expression.

die **Broochet**: The month of June.

der **Brunn**: Well. The importance of wells in Teutonic mythology cannot be understated. As a primary means of accessing water, wells provided a physical necessity. A well also appears in German mythology in the story of *Fraa Holle*. The well serves as the means for the heroine of the story to end up in Holle's realm. From the Urglaawe perspective, the well represents the path from life to death and from death to rebirth. Scandinavian lore also presents Mimir's Well as the font of knowledge in which Odin sacrifices his eye for wisdom (Larrington 7, Byock 24-25).

der **Bschluss**: Resolution. This is a resolution, most typically referring to conflict resolution or releasing a grudge. For a New Year's Resolution, see *Vorsatz*.

der **Butz**: Generally seen as an imp or as a mischievous field- or house-spirit, the Butz may also be beneficial, depending on his relationship with a particular human or humans. The English-language equivalent of this spirit is Puck. Deitsch folk songs (Frey 8) and poems also refer to der Butz by the name of Es Bucklich Männli, Buckliches Mennli, or Buckliches Männli (M. Graeff 20).

der **Butzemann**: The Butzemann is an activated scarecrow that is given the breath of life (Ochdem; see *Seel*) at *Grundsaudaag*. He is the "father" of this year's crop, and he guards his designated turf throughout the growing season. His formation is greeted with songs, and chants (Long 58, 59) as well as with flowers and other offerings.

Sometime between *Erntfescht* and *Alleliewezier*, the Butzemann is burned to represent sacrifices made by males for the good of the community. It is considered the height of bad luck to have a Butzemann standing beyond Allelieweziel. Quite a few scary stories surround a Butzemann whose soul went on the Wild Hunt with Holle, thus leaving a shell suitable for a baneful wight to use in order to wreak havoc.

A respected Butzemann, however, symbolizes and embraces the soul of the plant world around us. For an agricultural people such as the Deitsch, the Butzemann serves as a point of contact for *Blanzeschwetze*. His name, Butzemann, may reflect the beginning of a time of cleansing, both in the physical sense (of the hearth being cleaned on the day of his creation) and in a spiritual sense (the Butzemann takes with him the vanquished and banished aspects that we expel from our lives at Allelieweziel).

Another possibility for the origin of his name is in the related term "Butz," which would apply mostly for a Butzemann who is not burned prior to the onset of the Wild Hunt. Of course, both the "cleansing" and the "Puck" (see *Butz* above) origins may have validity.

Although in some places a "Butzefraa" (female scarecrow) has appeared (Long 55), the Braucherei traditions report that the scarecrow contains male energies in order to fulfill the seeding of the soil and the sacrifice at Allelieweziel.

die **Daaf**: Although this word is associated with Christian baptism, it is a term whose rightful meaning should be restored. The connotation of this word is that of sprinkling water, which is an old Heathen rite seen most clearly in the Anglo-Saxon Vatni Ausa. On the child's ninth night of life, the father sprinkles sacred water on the child's head and presents him/her with a name. The child is then presented to Frigg in Sege for protection.

It is interesting to note that Christian Continental German folk belief is that children who die prior to baptism are rendered into the care of Holle. It is not consistent with Christianity to include a heathen deity in a Christian religious rite. However, it is consistent with Heathenry that a child who passes away prior to (or even after) ceremonial naming would be taken by Holle.

daafe, gedaaft (verb): To sprinkle with water in a naming ceremony. See *Daaf*.

Deitsch (adjective, noun): Pennsylvania German; Pennsylvania Dutch. This endonym serves as the established term of ethnic identity of the descendants of immigrants who arrived between 1683 and the War of 1812 (some scholars include an ending year as late as 1820). The arrival sites may be as disparate as Philadelphia, Baltimore, New York, and other cities. Palatines and Swiss German migrants were the most numerous settlers, though Silesians, Moravians, and Swabians were also present in significant numbers. Some Hessian mercenaries also ended up assimilating into the Deitsch population. See *Deutsch*.

der **Deitschdaag**: Deitsch Day; Pennsylvania German Day; Pennsylvania Dutch Day. 6. Gehling, or October 6. Although organizers were already in Philadelphia prior to settlement, on this date in 1683, the first permanent settlers arrived from Krefeld to begin to lay the foundations of Germantown. The settlers originally dwelled in caves along the Delaware River.

While the first families were Christians (Mennonites and Amish), the subsequent waves consisted of people of all persuasions. Economic refugees were among the largest elements (Parsons 28). The British authorities eventually moved the settlers and filled the caves in due to the bawdy behavior of some of the Palatine settlers. The caves were around Front and Greene Streets in Philadelphia, and the bulk of them would now be beneath I-95, with the possible exception of the 200 block of Hancock Street in Philadelphia.

die **Deitscherei**: "Dutchery." This is a Deitsch word for Pennsylvania Dutch Country in Pennsylvania and contiguous areas in Maryland and Delaware. "Die Breet-Deitscherei" ("Broad Deitscherei") includes non-contiguous areas within Pennsylvania, New York, Delaware, Maryland, Ohio, West Virginia (Milnes 6-10), Virginia, North Carolina, Indiana, Illinois, Wisconsin, and Ontario. These areas consist of significant enclaves of communities that self-identify as Deitsch.

Deutsch (adjective, noun): German. Although the term "Deitsch" also means "German," it more specifically refers to the ethnic identity of the Pennsylvania Germans. Deutsch is the endonym drawn from standard European German that the Germans use for themselves. Thus, the term Deutsch is used by many when speaking Deitsch to refer to Germans elsewhere. See *Deitsch*.

der **Diener** (male); die **Dienerin** or **Dienern** (female): Clergy. This is a generic term and does not signify any particular faith or denomination. See also *Ziewer*.

es **Ding**: Thing. This was an historically annual (at least) gathering of the folk together to handle legal matters. This tradition, known as the Thing in English, survives in Iceland and is being revived within various Heathen sects. From the Urglaawe perspective, *Ziu* (Tyr) oversees the Ding. Urglaawe Sippschafts use this event to review and submit editions to bylaws, etc.

der **Distelfink**: Literally: Thistle Finch. Originally the stylized bird was modeled after the European Goldfinch (Carduelis carduelis), morphing over time to reflect the American Goldfinch (Carduelis tristis) and, occasionally, the unrelated Painted Bunting (Passerina ciris).

> *Just as the eagle came to symbolize America... so has the Distelfink come to symbolize... the Pennsylvania Dutch.* - Dr. Alfred L. Shoemaker (Drachman & Winston, 28).

With the exception of perhaps the groundhog, no animal is as closely associated with the Deitsch nation as the Distelfink. This stylized bird appears on folk art and on functional documents all across the Deitscherei and beyond.

While there are technical differences, particularly in color choices, in the artwork between the Distelfink and the similar Bird of Paradise, the two are often fused in the folk consciousness.

The Distelfink represents strong Luck, pride, and the very soul of the Deitsch nation. Folklore reflects and admiration of the ability of variety of birds in the Carduelis family to take what is considered waste or scrap (e.g., thistle seeds) by many other species and to use it to become successful. The Deitsch mirrored this behavior by migrating with almost nothing and building a new land.

es **Drankopfer**: Libation. Beverages consumed and offered typically include the following: mead (*Met*), ale (*Ael*), rob (*Garyel*), beer (Bier), apple cider (Abbelseider), apple juice (Abbelsaft), hard cider (Eppelwei), various herbal teas (Tee), or even water (Wasser) in a pinch.

es **Drinkhann**; plural: die **Drinkhanner**: Drinking horn. Less commonly used than a *Seidel* in Urglaawe, but very commonly used in wider Heathenry.

die **Dunkelhelft**: The Dark Half of the year begins on Allelieweziel (31. Gehling or October 31) with Holle's departure from the soil and onto the Wild Hunt. Holle governs this time of introspection and reflection. Allelieweziel serves as the start of the new spiritual year, as opposed to the calendar year, which starts on 1. Hadding, or January 1. The Dunkelheft ends on Walpurgisnacht, when Holle returns from the Wild Hunt.

der **Dunner**: Thor, thunder. Dunner is, perhaps, the most widely known of all Teutonic deities. Scandinavian lore is replete with stories of this god's actions.

In Deitsch lore, legends remain of Dunner's annual confrontation with three of the *Reifries*.

In Urglaawe, as in other Heathen sects, Dunner is widely considered to be the god of the "regular folks." His power and personality are seen in the booming thunder and the bright flashes of lightning. Heavy rains reflect his occasional outbursts of justified rage.

He is seen as the protector of beasts of burden and of production, particularly goats. From Scandinavian lore, we know that His means of transportation is a goat-drawn chariot. Oak trees (see *Eech*) are considered sacred to Him.

His name is the root of the name for Thursday in Deitsch (Dunnerschdaag) as well as in English. In the early Deitscherei, cattle were put out to pasture for the first time on Thursdays. Fogel (*Beliefs* 12) states that as late as the time of his writing (1915), cattle were not moved on Monday, Wednesday, or Friday. One may only speculate that cattle may be moved on Tuesday due to the day's connection to *Ziu*. Perhaps in a similar vein, wedding days also were most commonly scheduled for Tuesdays and Thursdays (see *Hochzich*).

Red is considered to be a color sacred to Dunner. Houseleeks (see *Hauslauch*), mountain ash, rowan, and oaks with red bark are associated with Him. The same applies to animals with red fur or coats. Even garments of red color could impart the power of Dunner. Thus, red flannel underwear is used to prevent rheumatism (Fogel *Beliefs* 12).

See also *Dunnerhammer, Dunnerkeil, Hammerbrauch, Hauslauch, Ruckschtee*.

der **Dunnerhammer**: The Thor's Hammer, known via Scandinavian lore as Mjölnir. This is a sacred physical object as well as a symbol of Thor's (*Dunner*'s) strength and power. The Hammer also is a symbol that represents all of Heathenry Gundarsson & Waggoner 21). See *Hammerbrauch*.

der **Dunnerkeil**: Thunderbolt. Deitsch farmers placed rounded stones (*Ruckschtee*) atop fence posts to form the shape of a Dunnerkeil around corrals. Although this practice almost died out since the time that Fogel described it in *Superstitions of the Pennsylvania Germans* (11), it was still done frequently enough for many folks to remember it into the present day. The Dunnerkeil, being sacred to *Dunner* (Thor), protects the cattle in the corrals.

der **Edelmut**: The ancillary virtue (see *Reenheide*) of Generosity is akin to the Heathen ethic of a "gift for a gift" as well as to the Hospitality of the Nine Noble Virtues. A generous act can initiate the reciprocity that builds community. One aspect to be considered is that generosity can certainly apply to instances in which the recipient does not have the means to provide a return gift of comparable value. Generous inclinations in the initial giving can avoid having the disparity become an issue in the gift exchange.

die **Edelreenheide**: Noble virtues. This is typically a reference to die Nein Edelreenheide, or the Nine Noble Virtues that are common across much of Heathenry. See *Reenheide*.

der **Eech**: Oak. Oaks in Deitsch culture are considered to imbue physical strength and healing power in those who touch them.

At least one Germanic tribe, the Chatti, is known to have held a particular oak tree sacred to *Dunner* (Padberg 41-42). The association of oaks with Dunner would certainly link them with physical strength.

Some Braucherei and Hexerei practitioners choose places of power near an oak (Milnes 83). The Mighty Oak ("der Mechdich Eech") hex sign (see *Schtannschild*) is the root of the symbol of Urglaawe. Patrick Donmoyer, of the Pennsylvania German Cultural Heritage Center at Kutztown University, has suggested that there might be a link between the Mighty Oak and the Helm of Awe, which appears in Icelandic (Gundarsson & Waggoner 22-23) lore, although he acknowledges that it may be impossible to ever prove such a relationship. However, the two symbols do share similar meanings.

See also *Irminsul*.

die **Eed**; plural: die **Eede**: Oath. As with other Heathen paths, oaths are taken very seriously. Typically, oaths are offered up at Sege or Sammel. One exception is the New Year's Resolution, which is set aflame on the wreath on New Year's Day. The resolutions are oaths that are taken either 1). to the self; 2). to the community; 3). to the deities. At the checkpoints throughout the year, one is to check whether the progress of the resolution is on target.

der **Eedring**: This is an oath ring, which is the item upon which oaths are taken in Urglaawe.

die **Ehr**: This is the Noble Virtue of Honor, which includes behaving in accordance with our words. Our Honor is reflected in our deeds. See *Reenheide*.

ehre (verb): To honor; to worship. Heathen connotations of "worship" focus on earlier meanings of the word from the Old English worthscipe, which means "worthiness." Thus the term is seen more as recognizing the "worth-ship" of the deities (see *Zieb*), wights (see *Wichde*), and ancestors.

die **Eil**: The owl, sacred to Berchta and known for its wisdom. Historically, among the Christian Deitsch, there was a malediction towards the depiction of owls in drawing or in print, and they were often associated with witches (a connection to Berchta) and cast in a negative light. An example of this would be how the owl in the folk tale of *Yorinde un Goringel* (Barrick *German-American* 109) flies into a grove and an evil witch then emerges. In the continuing paranoia of witches, owl carcasses were also nailed to the sides of sheds or barns in an attempt to frighten off other owls or to protect against evil spirits (Brendle & Unger 29).

Practitioners of Braucherei, however, never bought into this taboo against this "heathen" practice. The Eil is also the ninth new moon after Oschdre (the spring equinox) on the *Muunraad* and typically incorporates the time of the *Berchtaslaaf*.

Eileschpiggel, Til: Germanic trickster figure. Although the origins are uncertain, historians have tried to establish connections between this trickster and historical individuals. General consensus is that the stories appeared around the year 1300, but the roots probably run deeper than that. His name translates to "owl mirror," which perhaps reflects the reversal of traditional wisdom that Til Eileschpiggel represents. He is either

Lokian in nature or, a complete buffoon (Oppenheimer xxix), or a truth-teller (Barrick *German-American* 115), depending on the context of the tales. He was famous in Deitsch folklore for predicting the exact opposite of what would happen, and, with a semi-divine nature, people would follow his predictions and trouble would follow.

die **Eilaading**: Invitation. This is an invitation for a deity to be an honored guest at a ceremony.

der **Eisehannes**: Iron John. The "Wild Man" as depicted in Grimm's fairy tale "Eisenhans" has separate tales related to him within the Deitsch culture. In some tales, Eisehannes is regaining his lost socialization, while in others, he teaches harsh lessons to those who behave in an unfrithful manner (Leh, 7). Folk and fairy tales such as these continued to transmit the ancient Germanic worldview into successive generations after the conversion.

es **Elbedritsch**: Known by many name variations, this is a trickster figure in Deitsch lore, most innocently as the target of snipe hunts. In journeywork (see *Zeitschnur*), the Elbedritsch can mislead the worker or the client. Also, on the *Muunraad*, should a thirteenth new moon occur after Oschdre (the spring equinox), it is called the Elbedritsch moon.

der **Elbekeenich**, der **Erlkeenich**: "Elf-king." Despite the generally positive view of elves in Heathenry, the Deitsch term "Elbe" is sometimes used in compound words that carry a negative connotation (see *Elbedritsch*). Such is the case with this term (Simek 74). The Elbekeenich is mostly seen as a nefarious entity that appears very close to the time of one's demise. The Elbekeenich is seen to live in the branches of alder trees, which grow in generally inhospitable wetlands (Müller-Ebeling, Rätsch, & Storl 23).

Although some similarity may be seen between Albert Sterner's (ca. 1910) depiction called "The Erlking" and *Ewicher Yeeger*, it is highly unlikely that the Elbekeenich is the same entity as Ewicher Yeeger. The Elbekeenich is viewed negatively while Ewicher Yeeger, albeit feared, is viewed generally positively.

The Elbekccnich is perhaps best known through Goethe's 1782 poem entitled "Der Erlkönig." However, oral traditions regarding this entity are much older and exist also in Danish lore.

der **Elf**, plural die **Elwe**: Elf. The Elf is the equivalent of the álfr (plural: álfar) of Scandinavian mythology or the elves of Anglo-Saxon mythology. They are said to reside in Brechtelweheem, also called Elweheim (see *Lewesbaam*). Many modern depictions show the elves to be friends of mankind. Indeed, there are some indicators in lore that the spirits of some male ancestors may become álfar (Gundarsson *Volume. 2* 456).

There are hints, however, that elves are inclined to follow their own agendas and may not always be friendly towards humanity. In some cases, the effects of their actions can be detrimental to humans (Turville-Petre 232). Indeed, one term for "nightmare" in Deitsch, "Elbdraam," literally translates to "elf dream," and elves are seen as sometimes causing pains in humans (see *Elfschuss*).

Within the Deitsch culture, Elwe are most commonly known through their association as Santa's helpers. This is not the only reference to them, however. Some traditions of placing images of gnomes or elves in the garden have origins in creating a hospitable environment for local wights (see *Wicht*). In Urglaawe, Elwe have a general association with land fertility and a higher cosmic awareness.

der **Elfschuss**: Elf-shot. Gundarsson (*Volume 1* 460) describes the "alf-shot" as causing sudden sharp pains in humans and cattle. Grimm (180) makes connections between the Elves taking their shots and *Dunner*, concluding that the Elves are carrying out Dunner's orders. Brendle and Unger (*Witchcraft* 29) present a different, yet not inconsistent, connotation of the Elfschuss being an enchantment coming from a spirit, although not necessarily an Elf, who is independent of a human sorcerer. In this case, the spirit or wight could still be in the employment of a deity or an ancestor. This leads to a common Deitsch belief that the Elfschuss is an ancestor's (or deity's) attempt to gain the attention of the targeted human.

es **Entzicke**: Trance. A state of being that has origins in nearly universal shaman or oracle types of religious leaders (Yoder *Trance* 15), the trance is present in time-cord (see *Zeitschnur*) work. Indeed, even plain religious sects have had entranced preachers, indicating that the customs emerged from the pre-Christian era and continue into the present.

entzicke (verb): to entrance.

der **Erdgeischt**: Gnome. See *Zwarich*.

der **Erdschpiggel**: Earth-mirror. Belief into the present day is that children born with a caul are able to use a magic glass to locate money or treasure (Gehman 53).

es **Erntfescht**: This is the Harvest Home, or the original Deitsch thanksgiving (Yoder *Harvest* 3). While the Harvest Home is a traditional Germanic event with pre-Christian roots, it became also firmly ensconced in the Protestant churches as well. Within the context of both religions, members of the community would come together and trade specialty items among one another or ensure that families that suffered a death or a crop failure would have enough food to last them through the winter (Parsons 37-38). Similar community assistance projects, such as barn-raisings, are common even today in Deitsch culture. Urglaawe groups schedule annual food drives and donations for this event.

Ewicher Yeeger: The Eternal Hunter. Deity known to rescue the early colonists by driving game over the Blobarrick (Blue

Mountain/Kittatinny Ridge in Eastern Pennsylvania). Although He is considered a benevolent deity in nature, He is also on errands that exceed our understanding, and it would be easy for one to find himself beneath the hooves of His horse. He is considered to be a very old deity, perhaps even *Tuisto* Himself.

Despite early attempts to connect Ewicher Yeeger with *Wodan* via the concept of the Wild Hunt (Fogel 13), the sense that most reports of Ewicher Yeeger present an earth-borne feel to this powerful deity. In both Braucherei and Urglaawe, Ewicher Yeeger and Wodan are considered to be two very different gods. In Urglaawe, Ewicher Yeeger is considered to be of the *Wane* and is believed to be the consort of *Holle*.

A well-known depiction of Ewicher Yeeger is J. Allen Pawling's painting, *The Eternal Hunter*, as seen here in Graeff and Meiser's *Echoes of Scholla-Illustrated.*

Much like Heathens do not see *Dunner* (Thor) as the personification of thunder, we also do not see the reverberating sound that is associated with Ewicher Yeeger as being the Eternal

Hunter Himself. Instead, we perceive His power in the sound and in the memory of the successful settlement of the region. Thus, much like the natural phenomenon of thunder is explainable by science, so may Ewicher Yeeger's sound be attributed scientifically to a wind of warm air on the cold mountains or to flocks of migrating geese (Gehman 52). However, because the deity does not emanate from the phenomenon and vice versa, there is no conflict between the sensation of the deity's presence and the scientific understanding of the world around us.

See also *Allemaengel*.

der **Fagge**: Fain. A Fagge is a form of *Sege* that consists of the spoken word and presentation of various offerings. In return, the libations are imbued with the power of the honored deities. Meat offerings may be presented in a Fagge. This is in contrast to a *Blutvergiesse*, which would involve the sacrificial slaying of an animal.

die **Farewe**: Colors. In traditional Deitsch culture, colors have meanings and associations. Some of these associations are common in Hex Sign (see *Hexezeeche*) artwork as well as in other creative expressions. Certain colors, such as crimson, yellow-green, black, and white, are imporant in Urglaawe funerary rites.

Color	Fareb	Meaning
Black	Schwatz	protection, blending, binding, processing of soul between lives
Blood-red	Blutrot	blood, war, strife
Blue	Bloh or Blo	peace, calmness, peace, the sea, spirituality
Brown	Brau	earth, soil, friendship, steadfastness, strength
Crimson	Karminrot	Death, phase of passing on
Gold	Gold	glory, opulence
Gray	Groh or Gro	uncertainty, trickster, famine
Green	Grie	growth, fertility, ideas, bounty

Color	Fareb	Meaning
Orange	Aarensch	success in endeavors, extra energy (as with the Uruz rune)
Red	Rot	emotions, passion, lust, charisma, blood, phases of life, marriage. Also sacred to *Dunner*.
Slate	Schifferich	connection to minerals, rock
Tan	Gehlbrau	animals, connection to creation
Violet	Veilich, Purpel	sacred, cosmic, mystery, totality of the soul
White	Weiss	purity, power of the moon, flow of energy, illumination, rebirth
Yellow	Gehl	health in mind and body, connection to divinity and spirit, power of the sun, love of humanity
Yellow-green	Gehlgrie	commending to soil

die **Fasching**: Shrove Tuesday. The origins of Fasching, also known as the Faschtnacht and Mardi Gras, are almost certainly related to *Grundsaudaag*. The Heathen practices were originally tied to lunar calendar observances but eventually became associated with February 2. The timing of Shrove Tuesday comes from the Christian calendar and moves in accordance with the Computus' determination of the timing of Christian Easter.

In the Deitscherei, the most famous method of observing Fasching is the consumption of deep-fried doughnuts called Fastnachts or Faschtnachtskuche. The origin of this practice is almost certainly in Judeo-Christian Passover/Lent constructs.

While the observance of Fasching is far more subdued in the Deitscherei than in European countries, a hint of the connection between the Heathen events of Groundhog Day and modern Fasching may be found in Croatia's celebration of the Mesopust. On this holiday, which falls on Shrove Tuesday, a doll is constructed who is treated like a scapegoat for all of the bad things that happened during the prior year. This sounds very much like a *Butzemann*, except the Butzemann is honored rather than burdened, and the Butzemann takes vanquished habits and negative energies with him in fire on *Allelieweziel*.

While the Butzemann is typically created for Groundhog Day, it is not uncommon to have his creation occur later in the month. It is quite possible that the events of Mesopust and the Butzemann stem from the same traditions.

In the Deitscherei, another aspect of the Fasching is that the last person in the household to arise in the morning is deemed "the Faschtnacht," "der Faas," "der Faschingkluck," or myriad names. When I was growing up, within our household, the last child to arise in the morning of the Fasching had to do one extra chore by the end of the day. Customarily, in many Deitsch households, the last child has to tolerate teasing by his siblings all day long.

The same applies to the last child to arrive at school on Shrove Tuesday.

In the past, there were some rather elaborate teasing rituals involving the clucking sound of chickens in school. As the children arrived, the girls would cluck like hens and the boys would crow like roosters. As another child would arrive, he/she would receive instructions that he could not cluck or crow like the others until yet another child arrived. Instead, the last child would have to call out, "Hallo Faas!" to the next arriving child (Shoemaker 1-5).

If a child erred and clucked or crowed, there were penalties involved, particularly having to give a kiss to a member of the opposite gender. Girls, in particular, were encouraged to kiss any boy who caught their fancy.

The clucking, crowing, and kissing sound like they were originally part of some sort of fertility-related ritual. Teachers in the post-modern era would very likely be more than a little bit disquieted by their students engaging in this behavior. However, the tradition was clearly in effect well into the 20th century, and aspects of it may well live on in parts of the Deitscherei even now.

See also *Wildi Yacht*.

der **Folyer** (masc.); die **Folyerin** (fem.); die **Folyer** (plural): Fetch. This is the guardian spirit that attaches itself to one's soul (*Seel*) prior to (or at) birth and detaches itself at death.

The Folyer may appear as an animal or as a human spirit. Many traditions hold that the Fetch is of the opposite gender from the physical self. Experiences with the Fetches of various individuals in *Zeitschnurwaerrick*, however, have indicated that this is not always the case. In fact, work done in Braucherei to date has identified same-sex Fetches attached to men and women who identify as homosexual. Also, in one case, a woman also had two Folyer attached to her soul, and the result was a long history of disorientation and schizoid behavior.

The Folyer is often the portion of consciousness sent out to the other realms in journeywork and in ancestral and potential descendant contacts. The Folyer is also often credited in Braucherei with providing the senses of danger or impending doom. This is a function of the Folyer's role as guardian spirit.

It is also possible to lose one's Folyer through evil or irresponsible actions. The Folyer, as a living entity, is also subject to *Wurt*, and thus may choose to depart from individuals whose actions are detrimental to the Folyer's *Wurt* and future *Urleeg* (Wodening *Heathen Soul*).

die **Forrell**: Trout. On the *Muunraad*, the third new moon after *Oschdre* (the spring equinox) is the trout moon.

die **Frau Holle** (tale): The Grimm's Fairy Tale of *Mother Holle* or *Frau Holle* is considered a sacred text in Urglaawe. The story, which relates how a diligent girl enters Holle's realm when she falls down a well, is seen as a metaphor for the life, death, and rebirth cycle. The actions of the girl and of Holle reflect the importance of the ancillary virtues (see *Reenheide*) of Generosity (*Edelmut*) and Compassion (*Mitleid*).

The tale also contains insight into the rewards that hard work in one life can present to an individual's Urleeg and Wurt (see respective terms below) in a future life. Different versions bear variations of the details (Barrick *German-American* 110), but the overall moral of the story and the reflection of Wurt still apply. See also *Holle*.

der **Freibesitz**: Freehold or fellowship. This is an Urglaawe kindred that does not use oaths among the members.

die **Freindschaft**: Guild; lineage; family; guild of Brauchers and/or Braucherins. Guilds often can trace their "lineage" back many generations (Dickerson 39), with the training going from female to male to female to male, etc. (with the allowed exceptions of family members). The Freindschaft passes along the healing knowledge to the next generation of practitioners. It also provides some physical legacy objects as well as written and oral lore. While it is forbidden to write down some very few aspects of the oral lore, the vast majority of tales, legends, histories, and knowledge are now being made accessible to the next generation of Deitsch folks in the form of written materials. Among these materials concepts, writings, and theories that are highly relevant to Urglaawe.

der **Frey**: "Lord." A god of the Vanir (*Wane*) and the twin brother of *Freya*, He is best known from Scandinavian sources. Recognized as a deity of fertility, gentle rains, and abundance, traces of the awareness of Him live on in the traditional Deitsch New Year's fare. Sacred to Frey are the boar (whence comes the pork portion of the New Year's meal) and cabbage (represented by the sauerkraut in the meal). Scandinavian sources cite His father as Njörðr, who is known as "Nodd" or "Nadd" in Deitsch. Frey's holidays on the Urglaawe calendar are 1. Hadding (January 1) and *Hoietfescht*, though He is also honored at other times. Ann Gróa Sheffield's *Frey: God of the World* provides a great history and introduction to Frey. As Sheffield (1-3) points out, the association with fertility relates but one aspect of this very complex and multi-faceted god.

die **Freya**: "Lady." Freya is the twin sister of *Frey* and is also best known through Scandinavian lore. She is seen as the goddess of love, passion, sexuality, trance states (see *Entzicke*), shamanism, and journeywork. Cats and amber are considered sacred to Her. She is honored at various events throughout the Urglaawe year, most notably at *Hoietfescht*. For an excellent introduction to Freya, see Lafayllve's *Freyja, Lady, Vanadis*.

die **Frigg**: Best known from Scandinavian sources, Frigg is the wife of *Wodan,* mother of Balder, sister of *Volla* and *Phol*, and the matron of the *Ase*. She wards over the home and the hearth (see *Haerdziebin*), and She spins the fabric from which our *Wurt* is woven. She is also seen in the beauty of motherhood and in the entire realm of feminine creative energies. In Urglaawe, Her festival is 2. Hanning, or February 2. Birch trees and the Berkano rune are associated with Her. The spindle and the distaff are Her tools and are used in ceremonies honoring Her.

See also *Hochzich, Schpindelbrauch, Waerrickgawwel*.

der **Frosch**: Frog. On the Muunraad, the fifth new moon after Oschdre (the Spring Equinox) is the frog moon.

der **Fruchsfriede**: Fruchsfriede is the social order that compares to frith. Frith is described as the state of peace and the nature of social relationships conducive to peace (Tobin, *Praiseworthy* 15).

Despite the huge religious chasm dividing Urglaawe from the plain Anabaptist sects, many of the family, clan, and community structures of the latter are, quite possibly, retentions of earlier social order. For example, Amish society is very tribal, in some senses. They handle virtually all matters within their own communities. Children tend to grow up securely in a community that ensures interdependence and caring (J. Friesen, 144).

While all Heathen paths, including Urglaawe, celebrate individual achievement and success, the need for love, family, and community is paramount. Grönbech (13) describes Teutonic society as "a community based upon general unity, mutual self-sacrifice and self-denial, and the social spirit. A society, in which every individual, from birth to death, was bound by consideration for his neighbour." In a manner consistent with the adage "blood is thicker than water," kinship is valued more than personal elevation if the success will be to the detriment of kin.

An example of this importance is evident in *The Hildebrandslied*, wherein a son, Hadubrand, is about to engage in battle with a man who, unbeknownst to him, is his father, Hildebrand. Hildebrand asks Hadubrand about his lineage, and Hadubrand responds, saying that he did not know his father, but he was told that his name is

Hildebrand. Hildebrand attempts to avoid the battle and instead offers up gifts of gold arm rings. Hadubrand does not believe Hildebrand and accuses him of creating a ruse in order to win the battle. He then accuses Hildebrand of cowardice, thus compelling Hildebrand to engage in the battle despite the bonds of frith. The entire story is a tragedy. The death of Hadubrand is exacerbated by the fact that Hildebrand was put in a position in which he was forced to kill his own kin (Wood 4-11).

From the Urglaawe perspective, we owe Fruchsfriede to all humans simply by nature of our common existence. In considering our actions, though, we are to give consideration to our nuclear family first because we owe them the most Fruchsfriede. The next level of consideration goes to our extended family (including Sippschafts), then to our clans, our communities, our nations, and, finally, to all of humanity. All humans are deserving of the Fruchsfriede owed to them unless they break the peace through their actions. The bonds of frith also extend to the deities and to the wights around us.

Violations of Fruchsfriede may be corrected through spoken word or the offering of gifts or restitution. In the context of a repayment for loss of the life of kin or for stolen property, the payment was called weregild. Given our modern legal system, weregild in exchange for a life lost is not likely to satisfy the bereaved or the state. However, weregild for lost or damaged property is not unheard of within the Deitsch culture.

Within Fruchsfriede are several concepts that relate to the social aspects of human life: peace, security, gladness, order, structure, dignity, and *Gemietlichkeet*.

der **Fux**: Fox. On the *Muunraad*, the eighth new moon after Oschdre (the Spring Equinox) is the fox moon. As with the *Baer*, it is uncertain whether the timing of the Fux moon has anything to do with the fact that the fox was seen in some areas as a predictor of upcoming weather (Yoder *Groundhog* 53), similar to a groundhog. See also *Grundsau*.

die **Gans**: Goose. The goose is sacred to Holle and that relationship is highly likely to be the origin of Mother Goose. Additionally, it may also serve as the basis for a meal of goose at

Yuletide. The goose may relate to *Holle*, to *Berchta*, or to both. The connection to Holle comes through old German tales and references to snowfall as Holle shaking her goose-down bed, although some sources say eiderdown (Tatar 130). A stronger argument may be made for Berchta, who is described as having the foot of a goose (Grimm 281).

die **Garyel**: Cordial, rob. Typically made of elderberry, a cordial or rob is used as a libation in some Urglaawe rituals, particularly those honoring Holle. See *Drankopfer*.

der **Gebrauch**, plural - die **Gebreich**: Custom. This term bears the connotation of the folk customs and markers of the culture.

die **Gedderdemmerung**: Ragnarök or the Doom of the Gods, as viewed in Urglaawe, comes from the forces of chaos destroying this Universe (or Multiverse), which will result in the creation of a new Universe. It is similar in many ways to the Ásatrú concept of the end of this universe, but it differs in that (in Urglaawe philosophy), human souls are not, with exceptions, kept in the halls of the gods fighting battles daily in preparation of Ragnarök. Instead, humanity's purpose in life is to advance its consciousness in order to be a step closer to the current level of the deities in the next Universe. Thus, the cycle of life, death, and rebirth continues throughout this existence.

die **Gedechnisleicht**: A memorial service conducted in the absence of the physical body.

die **Gedechniszettel**: Braucherei tradition holds that any person who has a grievance towards (or unfinished business with) the deceased must make peace at the time of the funeral. One method (among several) states that the participant should place a coin into the gravesite or fire in order to close open wounds. Urglaawe has embraced this tradition but uses paper if a pyre is involved. The Gedechniszettel may also be used to express thoughts or feelings during the time of grief.

The participants are welcomed to write their resolutions to any conflict or to include any prayers or final thoughts on the paper. If the paper is folded, then the message is between that person and the deceased. If the paper is unfolded, then the message is among that person, the Ziewe, and the deceased. The papers may be tossed into the barrow or directly into the fire.

die **Gehling**: The month of October.

der **Geischt**: Ghost, spirit, a subset of the soul. See *Seel*.

die **Geischtlichkeet**: This is the ancillary virtue of Spirituality (see *Reenheide*). As is the case with many of the other ancillary virtues, Spirituality is not an aspect of one's disposition that can be created artificially. Thus, the pursuit of spiritual matters falls under this topic. The concept of Geischtlichkeet is more about the recognition of things beyond the physical self than it is about the actual experience of the divine.

es **Gemiet**: Mood, disposition, totality of Self. See *Seel*.

die **Gemietlichkeet**: This Urglaawe concept exceeds the typical dictionary translation of "coziness." Virtually every language has words that are difficult, if not impossible, to translate into a different language, which is why words are often adopted from one language into another. Some words reflect concrete items, such as insects that are native to a particular area or a legal process that is unique to a given country. Other words reflect concepts that are new or are unique to a given culture, such as the Polynesian system of tapu or kapu becoming (with some revision) known as "taboo" in English.

One Deitsch word that does not translate exactly into English is Gemietlichkeet (or Gemietlichkeit, depending on one's local variant of the language). This word is frequently translated as coziness, and that translation is certainly valid. However, there is a deeper aspect to the word that warrants more explanation.

Gemietlichkeet is also a state of belonging to everything and having everything belong to us. It is also a soul-satisfying joy or happiness that simultaneously emanates from and includes that state of belonging. Urglaawe philosophy holds that Gemietlichkeet is a primary goal for personal and community achievement.

A lack of a sense of belonging permeates much of our society in the current era. Very real circumstances force our attention to be focused on paying bills, finishing school projects, ensuring that our jobs skills are current (if we are lucky enough even to have a job!), worrying about the wars or politics, or any number of other issues that constantly bombard us. Many of us barely know our neighbors or are unable to spend a significant amount of time with loved ones. This disconnection from home, family, and community has led to numerous social problems about which all of us are most certainly already painfully aware.

Outside of taking prescription medications, what can be done about this situation? One seemingly simple answer comes to Urglaawe via Braucherei: attune your mindset with the time of year. During the time between *Walpurgisnacht* (April 30) and *Midsummer* (June 21), we are encouraged to revel in the joys of life. Celebrate the warmth of the sun on the land, the growth of the flowers or the crops, and the love of friends, family and Sippschaft. These are the wonders of life, and through deliberate, conscious living and embracing these joys we begin to set the foundations for incorporating a sense of Gemietlichkeet into our daily routines.

See also *Fruchsfriede*.

der **Getz**: Idol, statuary. Urglaawe altars include statuary or idols, whenever possible. While the idols are not considered to be the deities themselves, they serve as the focal point of the invocations. Thus, the deity may choose to occupy the statuary. Thus, the idols always treated with respect. Statuary can serve as objects of focus. The important thing to remember is that it is the deity who is honored, not the statuary.

die **Gewut**: The portion of the soul (*Seel*) that brings forth passions and emotions that inspire us to actions.

es **Glick**: Luck. In the context of Urglaawe, this is the portion of the soul (*Seel*) that accumulates and stores personal power.

die **Grabb**: Crow. On the *Muunraad*, the twelfth new moon after Oschdre (the Spring Equinox) is the crow moon.

der **Grundsau**: Groundhog. The groundhog is seen in Urglaawe as the messenger among the worlds. Due to the large number of openings in a groundhog burrow, the groundhog provided excellent mediating imagery to describe the Lewesbaam (world tree) and the portals to the other worlds. Also, on the Muunraad, the eleventh new moon after Oschdre (the Spring Equinox) is the Groundhog moon.

European German custom utilizes a badger instead of a groundhog in the role of prognosticator (Yoder *Grundsau* 52-53). See also *Baer*.

An entire new folklore has arisen around the Groundhog due to the entrance of Deitsch traditions into the wider American culture. Don Yoder (*Groundhog* 82-83) states that the Groundhog has become the symbolic or totemic animal of the Deitsch but without retaining the magical associations of the days of yore. Urglaawe's view of the Groundhog as a type of totemic animal is consistent with Yoder's view. However, most Urglaawer still retain a sense of magic or of spirituality within the Groundhog's retinue.

der **Grundsaudaag**: Groundhog Day. A major Urglaawe holiday that consists of the cleaning of the hearth, the honoring of maternal spirits (Idis) and female creative energies, the creating of the Butzemann, and the beginning of Spring Cleaning. On this day, the groundhog brings messages, predictions, and prognostications from the realms of the gods. For an agricultural people, the prognostication of the weather would be of high importance (Yoder *Groundhog* 43-44), which is very likely the reason that this aspect of the folk religion survived as it relates to the groundhog.

es **Gschenk**; plural: die **Gschenker**: Gift. Urglaawe adheres, as do most other Heathen paths, to the concept of a "gift demands a gift." (Hávamál : 145; Hyatt 61). Gift giving helps to build community and to strengthen bonds among neighbors (see *Schlachtzeit*). One exception to the gift giving is in circumstances that could result in an inadvertent curse. Negative energies can get imprinted upon a gift and become transferred to the recipient. Braucherei discourages the presentation of gifts during times of ill will, melancholy, or other negative emotional states. Instead, the giver is encouraged to engage a friend to present the gift by proxy.

For example, if a woman has recently suffered a miscarriage and has received a gift from another woman who is currently pregnant, the first woman's return gift could be imbued with the sorrow of her loss. That sorrow could make the gift toxic to the recipient.

Thus, it would be an act of frith for the first woman to ask her husband to fulfill the gift duty by proxy.

die **Hadding**: The month of January.

die **Haerdziebin**: The "Hearth Goddess," a kenning for *Frigg*.

Some old hearths and smoke houses in the Deitscherei have an image of a face in an eave just below the smoke vent. While some sources indicate that this may be the face of the Gnostic Sophia, particularly due to drawn portrayals of Sophia bearing a head with wings. There is some similarity between Frigg and Sophia, particularly when the aspect of cosmic wisdom is considered. However, Frigg is specifically associated with the home and the hearth.

The image above was provided by Patrick Donmoyer of the Pennsylvania German Cultural Heritage Center at Kutztown University.

der **Hammerbrauch**: The "Hammer Rite," which is performed using a physical hammer or by making the shape of a hammer over an object or area to be blessed. See *Dunnerhammer*.

der **Hammer-un-Sichel Brauch**: The "Hammer and Sickle Rite," despite the Soviet-era imagery involved in the name, is a sacred hallowing and blessing rite in Urglaawe. It is the most commonly used incantation in the hallowing of the altar during ceremony. See *Dunnerhammer*, *Hollesichel*.

die **Hanning**: The month of February. Outside of Urglaawe, the grammatical gender of this month is masculine (der), but linguistic sensibility and the feminine noun ending of the word substantiate the Urglaawe use of the feminine article (die).

der **Hauslauch**: Houseleek. Also called Gluck-un-Bieblin (Hens and Chicks), the houseleek is sacred to *Dunner* and is planted on the roof of the home to protect against lightning strikes.

der **Haussege**: House blessing. Urglaawe recognizes and incorporates the living Braucherei tradition of smudging and blessing homes and of placing charms and prayers at every entrance (Yoder *Hex Signs and Magical Protection of House and Barn*). See also *Zauberzettel*.

der **Heid** (male); die **Heidin** (female); die **Heide** (plural): Heathen (noun), a Heathen.

es **Heidetum**: Heathenry, Heathenism.

heidisch, Heidisch (adjective): heathen, Heathen (descriptive term).

heiliche, gheilicht (verb): To make sacred or holy.

die **Heiliching**: Hallowing. While all space is considered sacred in Urglaawe, the physical altar, statuary, and actual location where the deities are first invited to stand are consecrated using a Sickle, a Hammer, Distaff, Glove, or other implement.

der **Hein**: Grove, sacred ceremonial gronds. See also *Hof*.

der **Henschingbrauch**: The "Glove Rite," which is used to hallow the altar at the time of the Ding. Derived from Scandinavian lore, the glove represents the arm that *Ziu* (Tyr) sacrifices to bind the wolf Fenris, thus protecting Mannheem (the realm of humans).

die **Hex**: Witch, sorceress. See *Hexemeeschder, Hexerei, Zauberei, Zaubererin*.

der **Hexebaerrick**: Witches' Hill. This is a particular location along Witchcraft Road near Virginville, PA. Deitsch folklore relates that this location is a spot for the Witches Dances (see *Wonnetdanz)* of Walpurgisnacht and Moifescht. The location bears a strong similarity to *Allemaengel* and *Hexekopp*.

der **Hexedanz**: Fairy ring or Witches' Dance. The Hexedanz is a ring or circle where vegetation will not grow. It is often attributed to the presences of witches or fairies on *Walpurgisnacht*. See also *Allemaengel, Hexebaerrick, Hexefeld, Hexekopp*.

es **Hexefeld**: Witches' Field. Located approximately 3 miles west of Reamstown in Lancaster County, Hexefeld is another site associated with *Holle* and *Walpurgisnacht*. Reports of circles of footprints in the snowfall with no path leading to or from the circles have become part of the local folklore (Gehman 49).

der **Hexekopp**, der **Hexenkopf**: Witch's Head. Hexekopp, more commonly called Hexenkopf in English, is a mountain pillar located in Northampton County, PA. In Deitsch folklore (Heindel 66), it has a long history of spiritual activity, particularly on Walpurgisnacht. In a manner similar to Holle's journey to Mount Brocken in Germany (Rüttner-Cova 150), the Walpurgisnacht lore is associated with the return of Holle from the Wild Hunt. Hexekoppwasser, or water drawn from the hematite ore hole at Hexenkopf, is used to sanctify items that are placed on altars. See also *Allemaengel, Hexebaerrick*.

der **Hexemeeschder** (male): Sorcerer. See *Allemaengel, Hex, Hexerei, Zauberei, Zauberer*.

die **Hexerei**: Hexerei is a practice of folk magic or witchcraft with a long and convoluted history of differention from -- and similarity to -- *Braucherei*. In many regions of the Deitscherei, the difference between Hexerei and Braucherei lies in the intentions of the practitioner.

An oversimplified description of the difference would be that Hexerei's intentions increase the personal power of the practitioner at the expense of someone else while Braucherei's intentions are to heal the target or to build the community. The oversimplification within this concept can be seen in the following scenario:

A person has ringworm. He goes to a Braucher. The Braucher says an incantation over the infection and provides a remedy. From the person's viewpoint, the healer has conducted Braucherei. From the ringworm's viewpoint, the healer has engaged in Hexerei.

Similar scenarios can work in reverse wherein the Hexerei practitioner is conducting work that is more beneficial to a particular person while there are externalities among organisms or other entities. Braucherei and Hexerei are two sides of the same coin. In most areas of the Deitscherei, the terms are used with the intention serving as the differentiation. In other areas, the words are used interchangeably, or there is only one word or the other for the totality of both practices.

See also *Wille*.

der **Hexewolf** (sing.); die **Hexewelf** (plural): The Hexewolf (also called Hexenwolf) is a character in Deitsch legends. Much like the Jersey Devils wreak havoc across the Pine Barrens, the Hexewelf inhabit tracts of land across much of eastern Pennsylvania. Some folks say they are generally invisible, but they can manifest themselves in a visible form at will. Others say that they are not actually invisible, but, like a cuttlefish, are able to blend into their environment in an extremely effective way. Although those who claim to have seen it describe an animal similar to a Jersey Devil, the Hexewolf has never been said to have wings.

They are nocturnal creatures, perhaps baneful wights or spirits that have little use for humans, particularly humans' streetlights, headlights and flashlights. Thus, the Hexewelf tend to hunt at night and sleep during the day. However, crossing their path while they are hunting could be deadly. Even if you are not physically harmed, these creatures are said to be able to exert a dark force upon you, which leaves a blemish and plagues you with bad luck.

Many tales of the Lenape did not survive the Colonial era, so we will never know whether these are native creatures or whether they came over with the Deitsch settlers, hidden among their possessions.

They have been said to dwell in woods or meadows near Oley, on the ridges of Berks County, PA, by Cushion Peak, Eagle's Peak, The Pinnacle, and in Lancaster County along the Welsh Mountains. Some say they inhabit the woods atop Berks County's Mount Penn at the far end from the Pagoda, and on some nights hunt in packs, on two legs or on four. Not far from Angelica Lake, the wooded areas appear to be a favorite home. In the north, they are said to avoid the Blue Mountain Ridge, perhaps due to the presence there of *Ewicher Yeeger*, the Eternal Hunter, but on the other side of the ridge, in Carbon County, the stories re-emerge in the wooded areas just north of Mauch Chunk/Jim Thorpe.

Stories indicate that they occasionally appear as -- and let out howls like -- normal wolves; other stories say they have the ability to project their thoughts into the minds of those whose gaze they catch, and that is one way they stop their prey. They are said to have the power to render people and objects motionless with their gaze or with a single paw.

An interesting story, which sounds much like a Hexewolf, comes from farther west in Centre County, PA, in the late 1800's. The report involves "strange wolves" using a single paw to stop sleds full of lumber from being transported through Elk Creek Gap. The strange wolves were such a problem that some of the drivers began to paint hex signs (*Hexezeeche*) on their sleds (White 69). Eventually, the loggers simply stopped hauling lumber after sundown. Many believed the wolves were werewolves or were sent by a witch (*Hex*).

They have been rumored to ransack root cellars and garbage cans. They have also allegedly attacked livestock, chickens, but for some reason they do not attack dogs and cats. In fact, cats have been reported among their numbers on occasion, traveling comfortably with the pack.

es **Hexeschild**: Hex sign. See *Hexezeeche*.

es **Hexezeeche**: Hex sign. When on a barn, a hex sign is now commonly called a barn star (Scheierschtann). However, the symbols appear in numerous other areas of life, from birth certificates to wedding announcements to advertising to tombstones.

Despite numerous attempts both to diminish and to embellish the significance of these symbols, the full reality of the origins and meanings of them has yet to be wholly understood. Some Deitsch historians, particularly those with a Christian frame of reference, try to eliminate the existence of many Heathen symbols on the signs and describe them as being mere decorations. Particularly absurd are claims that the symbols only appeared shortly after the Civil War. Plenty of evidence contradicts that claim. On the other hand, some current-day

Heathen-oriented artists read significance into signs of previous eras that may not be altogether true.

The reality probably falls somewhere in between both viewpoints. There is no doubt that many of the symbols on the signs are thousands of years old (Donmoyer 17) and of Heathen origin and have meaning to people who understand the original or current conventional meaning of the symbols.

However, it cannot always be determined whether the artists who created the works of yesteryear actually put their intentions behind the symbol's conventional meaning. Thus, the meaning may be stronger in the eye of the beholder than in the hand of the creator. In other cases, though, we have record of some of the thoughts of the artists or of those who commissioned the work. In some of those cases, there is clearly a belief in the power of the symbols and the signs (Yoder & Graves 58-59).

The re-emerging use and importance of these symbols in Urglaawe and in German Heathenry is resulting in an increasing accessibility to the creators' purposes and intentions. While we cannot always be certain of the intentions of the past, we can have better insight going forward. To Urglaawer (and to a significant percentage of the Deitsch), the signs are symbols of hallowing and protection. This is a view seen in wider Heathenry, also (Gundarsson & Waggoner 23).

The study of the symbols and signs on barns and other objects is an ongoing effort, and more information will most certainly follow.

der **Hoch**: The Higher Self. See *Seel*.

die **Hochzich**: Wedding. Numerous deities, including *Frigg, Dunner, Waahr,* and *Ziu* are seen as overseers of weddings. Gundarsson (*Volume 2* 271) states that, perhaps due to its association with Frigg, Friday is the best day for a wedding. This viewpoint is supported by Fogel's (*Beliefs* 17) statement that Friday is the luckiest of days due to its relationship with Frigg and is, therefore, a most favored wedding day.

Interestingly, though, Fogel also states (*Beliefs* 11) that Tuesday and Thursday are the most favored weddings days in the Deitsch counties due to their associations with Dunner and Ziu. If Fogel is correct in this theory, then this is one Heathen tradition that lives on very strongly within the Plain (Amish, Mennonite, etc.) communities, although the original reason for choosing those days is almost certainly lost to the participants.

Brides traditionally wore red, presumably Dunner's favorite color (Guerber 56) and a color that is also associated with Ziu. This is a jolting change from the purity associated with white wedding gowns in modern American society.

der **Hof**: Courtyard. Ceremonial grounds. See also *Hein*.

die **Hoiet**: The month of July. Traditionally, the Hoiet was the haymaking time that fell at varied times in mid-July into August.

es **Hoietfescht**: Literally meaning the "festival of the hay time," Hoietfescht is the celebration of the first harvest and the haymaking. It derives its name from Hoiet (July) and falls in the last week of July or the first week of August.

es **Hokekreiz**: Fylfot, swastika. The "hooked cross" has long been dogged by the misuse and abuse perpetrated upon it by the Nazis. However, Heathens of all types have been reclaiming this ancient symbol for use within the proper religious and spiritual contexts. Hilda Ellis Davidson (83) theorized that symbol might have been associated with Thor (*Dunner*), perhaps representing His Hammer. She also suggested that it might be related to a Bronze Age sun cross. Both theories are consistent with the perception of the symbol in Deitsch culture. The symbol is most frequently seen as a Swirling Swastika (Yoder & Graves 28, 33, 67) in barn stars or hex signs (see *Scheierschtann*).

An example of the Swirling Swastika can be seen in a sign that is commonly called the "rain hex." This barn star reflects a wish or blessing for an appropriate amount of rain, thus also implying an appropriate amount of sun. Heavy rains are associated with Dunner, thus sustaining the possibility of a connection between Him and the symbol.

die **Holle**, die Fraa **Holle**: Holle is one of the most well known goddesses in Braucherei and is, perhaps, the principal patroness of Urglaawe. In Germanic lore, She is seen in the falling snow and in the power of whirlwinds. She is seen as a compassionate goddess (see *Mitleid*) who also demands order in the home.

Holle guides the cycle of life, death, and rebirth in all areas of existence. She oversees that cycle in humans as well as in the earth. Thus, in modern times, the Jera rune (see *Roon*) is associated with Her.

In Hessia, a pond, known as Frau-Holle-Teich, features a beautiful statue of the goddess in a serene meadow. Mount Brocken is said to be Her holy place in Europe, much as *Hexenkopf* is Her home in the Deitscherei.

Urglaawe tradition, stemming from Braucherei oral lore, constructs the calendar of the spiritual year around Holle's activities. The spiritual calendar begins on October 31 (see *Allelieweziel, Dunkelhelft*) with Her departure from this physical plane. In Urglaawe, Holle is seen as the leader (or sometimes a leader, along with Wodan) of the Wild Hunt (*Wildi Yacht*) and engages in numerous parades involving an entourage of spirits (Chisholm 74).

Holle returns from the Wild Hunt on April 30 (See *Walpurgisnacht*). An oral tradition from Braucherei states that we are to open all doors and windows on that night in order to make it easier for Holle to inspect the home. Her return heralds the beginning of the Bright Half of the year (see *Brechthelft*).

Holle has always been an active presence in the practice of Braucherei, particularly when the healing work involves a lost spirit, soul, or entity.

Holle is of the *Wane* and is thus often compared to the goddess Nerthus. However, the god Njörðr, also known as Nadd, or Nodd, is not seen as a consort of Holle. Instead, Holle is believed to be the consort of *Ewicher Yeeger*. The perception of this relationship could stem from the relative proximity of the Blobarrick (see *Ewicher Yeeger*) to Hexenkopf.

Although Urglaawe recognizes the god named Holler from Scandinavian lore, there is no clear relationship between Holle and Him at this time.

See also *Aldi Fraa*, *Frau Holle* (tale), *Gans*, *Hollebeer*, *Hollesichel*, *Miehl*.

die **Hollebeer, Hollerbier**, other spelling variations: Elder, elderberry. Sacred to *Holle* (Müller-Ebeling, Rätsch, & Storl 43) and bearing Her name, the elder bush is viewed as a spiritually protective plant.

die **Hollesichel**: Sacred tool of the goddess *Holle* (Grimm 476), the sickle, along with the *Dunnerhammer* (Thor's Hammer) is a commonly used tool for the consecration of an altar. The sickle also is the primary symbol of Urglaawe.

die **Holzent**: Wood duck. On the Muunraad, the second new moon after Oschdre (the Spring Equinox) is the wood duck moon.

der **Holzhaahne**: Woodcock. On the Muunraad, the first new moon after Oschdre (the Spring Equinox) is the woodcock moon.

der **Hottenstein** ("holy rock"): This is the rock in the Spessart Forest in Germany from which Frankish law was dispensed in an annual Ding starting, at the latest, in 380 CE.

die **Idis**; plural: die **Idise**: An Idis is a matriarchal spirit who watches over the progression of her clan. The terminology has been lost within Deitsch culture, so "Idis" is a backformation. However, we do find remnants of concepts regarding deceased ancestors serving as guardians. Stories, legends, and folk tales of "guardian angels" and "fairy godmothers" bear some traits in common with both the Idis and the *Walkyrie*. However, the clearest descriptions and presentations of these entities come to us from Scandinavian lore.

der **Irminsul**: The Irminsul serves as a symbol of Germanic Heathenry. Urglaawe includes the modern conception of this pillar as a depiction of the Tree of Life (Yggdrasil: See "Lewesbaam).

Theories abound as to the ancient significance of these symbols. Among the theories is that the Irminsul is an all-sustaining universal pillar, which would be consistent with the Tree of Life. Urglaawe hypothesis (community gnosis unsubstantiated by lore) is that the Irminsul is sacred to Ziu (Tyr) or to Tuisto.

die **Iwwerliefering**: Tradition, legacy, heritage.

der **Landauer** (male); die **Landauern, Landauerin** (female); die **Landauer** (plural): Originally meaning "an inhabitant of Landau" in the Palatinate, a current connotation of the word refers to one who surmounts tremendous obstacles and achieves his/her goals or makes a name for him- or herself. There is a maverick or defiant sense to this word, also, which generally is a reflection of those who stood up to oppressive civil and church authorities in the past. This sentiment seems to have originated in a 1724 Palatinate law prohibiting emigration to Pennsylvania (Mutzbauer 137, 141-142).

die **Leich**, die **Leicht**: Body, corpse. Both terms mean the shell of a deceased person, but both also have a more general, though less frequently used, meaning of "body." For Urglaawe purposes, "Leich" refers also to the physical body as it applies to soul lore (see *Seel*) while "Leicht" carries the more common connotation of the deceased.

es **Leichtfeier**: Funeral pyre. This is a preferred, though not yet legal, way for the disposal of the physical body in Urglaawe.

der **Leichtlaaf**: A funerary procession. The procession passes through the crowd of particpants, who may say their prayers or toss their memorial tickets (see *Gedechniszettel*) into the barrow (see *Barick*).

die **Lenzbutzerei**: Spring cleaning, beginning on *Grundsaudaag* and to be completed by *Walpurgisnacht*.

die **Lenzing**: The month of March.

der **Lewesbaam** or **Lewebaam**: The Tree of Life, Yggdrasil. Although a few variations exist in Braucherei of the nature of the Lewebaam (Sicher 6, 16), Urglaawe reconciles the Heathen aspects of the variations with extant sources, particularly the *Poetic Edda*. Although the vast majority of Urglaawer ascribe to the nine "worlds" view, a second cosmology, consisting of nine "regions," is also described below.

Nine Worlds Cosmology

In the Teutonic worldview, the Tree of Life is the mediating imagery used to describe the relationship and the location of the Nine Worlds (Die Nein Welte). The imagery continued after the Heathen era and even appears on some modern Hex Signs (see *Schtanneschild*), albeit often (as depicted on Jacob Zook's *Tree of Life* sign here) with a number of worlds that is inconsistent with the Heathen tally.

The names of the Nine Worlds in Urglaawe are as follows. Please note that most of these names are neologisms drawn from names cited in Scandinavian lore.

Aseheem or Aseheim -- Known from Scandinavian lore as Asgard, the home of the deities of the Ase (Aesir) tribe.

Waneheem or Waneheim -- Vanaheim, the home of the gods of the Wane (Vanir) tribe. Waneheem is known in Braucherei also as Himmelgegend.

Mannheem or Mannheim -- Midgard, the realm of humanity.

Rieseheem or Yotunheim -- Jotunheim, which is the realm of the Giants (Riese) in Scandinavian lore.

Schwatzelweheem or Zwarichheim: The home of various entities, such as the dark elves or dwarves.

Brechtelweheem or Elweheim: The home of the light elves.

Helheem or Helheim: The realm of the dead.

Muspelheem or Feierheim: The realm of primal fire.

Newwelheem or Newwelheim: The realm of primal fire.

Nine Regions Cosmology

Another depiction, described by Lauren Sicher (6, 16), consists of the following regions ("Gegende") and aspects of the Lewesbaam:

Hohegegend: The Realm of Divinity.

Himmelgegend: The Realm of spiritually advanced ancestors (see also *Elf, Idis*).

Hatzholz: Realm of the physical plane. This is the wood of the trunk of the Tree of Life and is the visible world in which we live.

Unnergegend: Realm of earth-based spirits and evolving ancestral spirits who are waiting to be reborn. This realm is located at the upper roots of the tree.

Dunkelgegend: Realm of destruction and transformation.

There are also four directions for the leaves of the tree; these make up the additional four regions, thus resulting in a total of nine.

Naddbledder (North Leaves): Place of ice.

Suddbledder (South Leaves): Place of fire.

Oschtbledder (East Leaves): Place of magic.

Weschtbledder (West Leaves): Place of spiritual journeys.

There are other cosmologies in Braucherei. Despite the differences in location and nomenclature, however, all of the reported views share similar features, including the concept of humanity living in the center of the universal existence. The oral lore regarding the Lewesbaam is currently undergoing additional study and review; thus, more information may emerge regarding the understanding of the practicing Brauchers who utilize these living concepts in the present day.

es **Lewesraad**: Cycle of life, death, decay, rebirth. Urglaawe sees all of existence in a pattern of cycles, or, perhaps more precisely: spirals. This view, as it pertains to crops and herds, is shared across much of Deitsch society, regardless of religion. It is a core component of the culture of the Amish and other plain sects (J. Friesen 140). In Urglaawe, however, the concept includes the cycle of the individual, the soul, the universe, and all of existence. *Holle* is the keeper of the order of the cycles in the current universe, with *Frigg* and the Norns (see *Wurthexe*) executing the progression of time, space, and Wyrd (see *Wurt*).

es **Leweszeeche**: Thew, conduct of living. This term denotes the commonly accepted social markers and behaviors within a given culture.

die **Megge**: See *Seel*.

der **Meind**: The mind. Also the portion of the soul (see *Seel*) that carries memories and brings forth ancestral qualities.

die **Menschepflicht**: Moral duty; thew. This is a term for the obligations that a member of any community or society has to others. The obligations reflect the culture of the community in question. See also *Fruchsfriede, Verwalting, Zusaagpflicht*.

Merseburg Incantations: Two charms that reflect the spoken word among the ancients in a manner similar to modern *Braucherei*. The First Merseburg Charm is a releasing charm, which is meant to unfetter prisoners (Simek 84). The Second Merseburg Charm is a healing charm and includes the names of several deities. The scene described in the Second Merseburg Charm appears in depictions on bracteates from the 5th and 6th centuries (Simek 278). Although the relationship among the deities is in dispute, the existence of the charms is important in establishing the core of Braucherei being of Heathen-era origin. Similar chants and incantations may be found in other Teutonic areas as well (Sheil *Old Norse Charms* 2-5).

der **Met**: Mead. Mead is the sacred drink of Wodan and is used in many Urglaawe rites. See also *Drankopfer*.

der **Midsummer**: The summer solstice and ceremony to the goddess Sunna. This event is considered to be a time of joy and celebration.

die **Miehl**: The Mill. Envisioned location whither Holle takes the souls of the departed in order to process them for rebirth. Although other locations are sometimes reported, this is the most common one known to us from time-cord (see *Zeitschnur*) work as well as from oral tradition.

es **Mitleid**: This is the ancillary virtue (see *Reenheide*) of Compassion. The concept is different from the modern era understanding of this word, however. The focus of Mitleid is that of an appropriate compassion for others who are in a position through no fault of their own or who have seen their errors and are attempting to correct them. Compassion for irresponsibility is detrimental to the whole of the community. However, equally detrimental is providing no path to redemption for those who are trying to straighten themselves out. They become stuck in a quagmire of their mistakes, even if they are striving to distance themselves from their prior behavior.

In some cases, the compassion is towards those who have experienced a loss or a tragedy. This may include a loss of employment or losses incurred in a natural disaster, etc. Each year, Urglaawe organizations hold a food drive at Erntfescht. Filling the local food banks can help the wider community. These are gifts in exchange for the gifts we have in our lives. They are voluntary and free of compulsion. Also, we never know whether we may be in need of such assistance ourselves someday.

We should take careful consideration of the errors or crimes and the efforts the individual is taking to correct his/her ways. Mitleid can result in our lending a hand, when feasible in order to help strengthen our community overall.

The folk tale of *Frau Holle* provides some insight into the Germanic understanding of the importance of Mitleid. The mistreated stepdaughter falls into a well and awakens in Holle's meadow. The girl encounters some bread that is baking in an oven and will soon burn if not removed. The girl dutifully removes the bread. She then encounters an apple tree, the branches of which are heavy with apples. The girl shakes the tree to lighten its load. Holle rewards these compassionate acts, along with other virtuous behavior, by covering the girl in gold before sending her back to her family. Conversely, her lazy stepsister, who lacks virtue consistently throughout the tale, is covered in pitch.

es **Moifescht**: See *Wonnetdanz*.

Mountain Mary: Circa 1749-1819. Known in Deitsch as "die Barricke Mariche" and in German as "die Berg Maria," Anna Maria Jung (or Jungin with the feminine suffix) is considered the patroness of Braucherei among the Deitsch. Although reports vary regarding the details of her life, it is known that she was a Swabian from Württemberg. Her family fled to Philadelphia prior to the American Revolution, arriving in Philadelphia in 1768 or 1769 (Brown 10-15).

Mary lost her entire family to the plague while sailing from Amsterdam to Philadelphia (Brown 11). She eventually met and married a man named Theodore Benz, who died during the American Revolution. After his death, Mary never remarried and became a recluse who was dedicated to spiritual matters and to healing. She was reputed to have tended a magical herb garden (Kriebel 100), and she is credited with establishing the Oley Freindschaft Braucherei guild.

Although Mountain Mary was Christian, at least nominally if not devoutly, there is no question that a significant body of Heathen oral lore survived in the current era due to her contributions and efforts. Therefore, it is most fitting that Urglaawer honor her among the ancestors and the heroes of the path.

die **Muddernacht**: "Mother Night" is the first night of Yuulzeit (Yuletide), which starts at sundown on December 20 (Urglaawe "days" begin at sundown, e.g., Wednesday begins at dusk on Tuesday) and begins the celebration of the Winter Solstice. Tradition holds that this is the night in which Sunna, the deity of the sun, is spiritually reborn.

die **Mumming**: A depiction of the Wild Hunt (*Wildi Yacht*) that typically takes place around the New Year. Mumming includes a parade of costumed people who stop at homes to recite New Year's blessings. The Mummer's Parade in Philadelphia is an offshoot of this tradition (Milnes 184-185). See also the Belsnickeling practice under *Yuul*.

der **Mut**: This is the Noble Virtue (See: "Reenheide") of Courage. Heathenry requires a lot of personal strength to complement the other virtues. Trying to change the world and to advance the human life wave requires energy, strength, and valor. Without courage, nothing gets accomplished.

es **Muunraad**: The Moon Wheel. This is the Deitsch "moon zodiac," which contains twelve annual signs plus one additional sign, if there should there be a thirteenth new moon in a single year. The full range of astrological uses of the Muunraad is still being researched, but it is known through two different Braucherei Guilds (see *Freindschaft*) to be a guide to planting and harvesting as well as an indicator of animal or human dispositions (Tobin, *Es Pennsilfaanisch Muunraad* 4, 8-9).

The names of the Muunraad signs throughout the Deitscherei are not always consistent with the Deitsch names in the Guilds' traditions. In some areas, the old names were lost and the more conventional zodiac names were used to identify the Muunraad signs. However, the large body of oral and written lore reflects a common folk tradition concerning the significance of the signs to the planting, purging, healing, and harvesting (Barrick *Moon-Signs* 41-43).

See also *Aadler, Baer, Eil, Elbedritsch, Forrell, Frosch, Fux, Grabb, Grundsau, Holzent, Holzhaahne, Schillgrott, Schpeecht.*

die **Neigierheit**: "Neigierheit" literally means "curiosity." Curiosity, as an ancillary virtue (see *Reenheide*), relates to a general desire to know more about life and existence. Being a Seeker of truth is a high calling in Braucherei and complements the ancillary value of Spirituality. Information is power, and learning the mysteries of the world, of the universe and of existence empowers our communities and advances human consciousness.

die **Nein Welte**: See *Lewesbaam*.

die **Newwereenheide**: Ancillary virtues. Many of these ancillary virtues are conditions and are not aspects of one's disposition that can be forced or created without an expansion of consciousness. Thus, the seeking or the undertaking of effort to embrace or to understand these virtues is as important as the virtues themselves. See *Reenheide*.

die **Newweling**: The month of November.

Nine Sacred Herbs: While *The Lacnunga* described the nine herbs sacred to the Anglo-Saxons, the Deitsch have their own sacred nine. Three come from wood (dogwood flowers, elder blossoms, wintergreen). Three come from the fields (Fimf-Fingergraut or cinquefoil, catnip, ground ivy), and three from the garden (horehound, sage, and thyme). Another way to view these is three herbs, three vines, and three shrubs (Hess, *Nine Sacred Herbs* 10). In Urglaawe, these herbs are gathered after 15. Wonnet (May 15).

der **Ochdem**, der **Odem**: Breath; the breath of life. This is the gift of Wodan bestowed upon humanity at creation. See also *Seel*.

es **Opfer**: Offering. An offering made to a deity, wight (see *Wicht*), or ancestor.

die **Ordning**: Order; thew. Ordning is a Deitsch word that is used in various religious contexts to the law or the order of the congregation. Within Urglaawe, the term applies to the social conduct as delineated in the oaths of a Sippschaft.

See also *Ufffassing*.

der **Oschdraslaaf**: This is the progression or procession of Oschdra, which takes place on the vernal equinox (See: "Oschdre"). Oschdra's image is paraded from fields or the gardens to the altar for ceremonial honoring.

die **Oschdre**: Oschdre is the vernal equinox and the celebration of the goddess Oschdra. Interestingly, "Oschdre" is a plural word, so there is some sense of it having been a multiple-day or multiple-event observance in the past.

die **Oschdret**: The month of April.

die **Pflicht**: This is the thew of Duty. Per the concept of *Fruchsfriede*, all of humanity bears the responsibility of being good social citizens. Beyond the common responsibility of all humans, the nature of an individual's Pflicht depends partially on one's family and one's role within the community. For example, a farmer would have different duties (to deal fairly with consumers, to provide quality product) from a sanitation worker (to remove waste, to uphold privacy, etc.). However, one's Pflicht requires that one do the best job that he or she can and that all parties treat others fairly.

der **Phol**, der **Voll**: Originally conjectured to be *Balder*, but now considered a separate deity of the *Ase*. Phol is mentioned in the Second Merseburg Charm (see *Merseburg Incantations*), and, according to Simek (256), it is not likely that Phol is Balder. Instead, Simek believes that Phol is the brother of the goddess *Volla* (known as Fulla to the Scandinavians). In Urglaawe, Phol is viewed as the brother of Volla, and is thus also the brother of Frigg. In Deitsch, the spelling "Voll" is more common and reflects the sibling relationship with Volla.

die **Pilyerrees**: Pilgrimage. The Oley Freindschaft (guild of Brauchers) conducts a pilgrimage to the grave of *Mountain Mary* in Pike Township, Berks County, PA. The pilgrimage takes place on the Sunday closest to November 11, which is the presumed date of Mountain Mary's birth. The pilgrimage typically is just over two miles long, though there have been longer pilgrimages from Pikeville, PA, to the graveyard.

der **Queschtbaam**: Maypole. See *Wonnetdanz*.

es **Raad**: Wheel. This is the circle of leaders of a Braucherei guild or of an Urglaawe kindred.

die **Reenheide**: Virtues. Urglaawe recognizes and accepts the Nine Noble Virtues (Die Nein Edelreenheide) that are embraced in most of Heathenry. These virtues include the following:

die *Addning*: Discipline
die *Ausdauer*: Perseverance/Steadfastness
die *Ehr*: Honor
der *Mut*: Courage
die *Schaffichheit*: Industriousness
es *Selbschtzuverdraue*: Self-Reliance
die *Treie*: Fidelity/Troth
die *Uffwaarting*: Hospitality
die *Waahrheit*: Truth

Implied among these, but more directly state in Urglaawe, are ancillary virtues called Newwereenheide:

der *Edelmut*: Generosity
die *Geischtlichkeet*: Spirituality
es *Mitleid*: Compassion
die *Neigierheit*: Curiosity
der *Selbschtreiguck*: Introspection
die *Selbschtverbessering*: Self-Improvement
die *Verwalting*: Stewardship
die *Verwandschaft*: Kinship
die *Weisheit*: Wisdom

A description of each virtue is presented in its respective Deitsch alphabetical location in this dictionary.

die **Regel**: Rule, thew. This term has not appeared in regular Urglaawe discourse as of the time of this writing. However, it is a common Deitsch word relating to rules of all sorts, including legal rules, codes of conduct, etc.

der **Reifkeenich**: King Frost, who represents the onset of the winter. There is a resurging practice of railing against him with during the first week of *Newweling* (November).

die **Reifries**: Frost Giants (see *Ries*), a race of antagonists to the deities. Best known are the three Frost Giants of the month of *Wonnet* (May). These Giants names are Dreizehdax, Vatzehvedder, and Fuffzehfux (Tobin, *Walpurgis Nacht* 6). Each is beaten back by the god *Dunner*.

die **Reiniching**: Cleansing. This is a traditional Deitsch act that is the final function of a funeral rite, and it directly involves the person (or people) who were the closest kin or who were most directly impacted by the loss. Birch branches or twigs are collected, sometimes by one of the people most directly impacted by the death, and are decocted into a strong tea. The tea cools during the funeral or memorial rite. As the end of the rite approaches, a portion of the decoction is distributed among the folk. It may be either drunk or drawn in runes on the foreheads of the participants. The following morning, the remainder of the decoction is poured on the impacted individuals, along with blessing chants and prayers for the living. Tradition is for the volume of the tea to be sufficient to "douse" the shock of the loss (not to douse the grief per se, though).

die **Richtschnur**: Scruples, guideline, guiding principle, thew. This term relates to the explicit or the inexplicit - yet understood - parameters of the values of a community or society.

der **Ries**: A Giant. The Giants are proto-conscious beings who often stand in opposition to the gods. However, although there are plenty of stories in Scandinavian, Anglo-Saxon, Continental German, and Deitsch lore about conflict between the gods and the Giants, there is also ample evidence that the gods often mated and procreated with Giantesses. It is also not unheard of for a goddess to take a giant as a husband; for example, Gefjon (Gewwern) had four sons by her Giant husband. See *Reifries*.

die **Roon** (pronounced to rhyme with "tone"); plural - die **Raane**: Rune. The runes have been known to Brauchers since time immemorial. However, it is not clear whether all runes were consistently used or whether some runes were more prominent than others. Most often seen are Hagalaz (in this case, especially from the Younger Futhork), Ingwaz, Naudhiz (used to seal wounds and bless bruises), Sowilo, Gebo (used to close healing sessions), Uruz (to imbue the client with extra energy), and Laguz (to tap into the collective unconscious). See also *Holle*.

Runes may also be at the root of some hex signs (*Hexezeeche*). For example, six-pointed rosette, which is widely considered to signify banishing, may have its roots in the Hagalaz rune of the Younger Futhork (Donmoyer *Hagal* 9).

There are many excellent resources for runes available online and offline. The runic training for several members of Distelfink and Hottenstein comes from the Denali Institute of Northern Traditions (http://www.runesbyragnar.com) and from numerous books by Edred Thorsson, Freya Aswynn, and Diana Paxson.

die **Roonfaahne**: Rune banners. Rune banners are used frequently in Urglaawe. Colors employed are typically those of hex sign color conventions, but funerary rite banners employ a combination of the hex sign convention and Braucherei colors.

The red (death) banner bears a white (freeing of energy) Raidho rune, representing the great journey.

The green banner bears a yellow Jera rune. Braucherei utilizes either yellow or green to represent the physical body's return to the Earth. This aspect also contains a "loose soul" concept, meaning that the physical body and the ethereal body are separated, with (at least) one part of the soul continuing on its journey. In hex sign conventions, the yellow also represents the connection to the divine. The Jera, in this case, represents the stage of the life cycle. In Urglaawe lore terms, this is the reaping by Holle.

The black (transition) banner bears a white (free-flowing energy) Kenaz rune. This represents the mystery of transformation, the ongoing fire of the soul, and the casting of light before the soul on its journey to Holle's Mill.

The white (rebirth, free-flowing energy) banner contains a blue (spirituality) Ingwaz rune. This represents the germination of the eternal part of the soul into a new body.

der **Ruckschtee**: Rounded stones placed on fences to protect cattle. A Ruckschtee was also placed under the pillow to prevent insomnia. Fogel (*Beliefs* 11) describes the Ruckschtee as a reflection of Dunner's hammer, Mjölnir. See also *Dunnerkeil*.

der **Saal**: This term is used for an Urglaawe temple or meeting hall.

es **Sammel**: "Gathering." Similar to the Ásatrú and Theodish sumble, this is the community gathering in which participants share their thoughts, oaths, wishes, blessings, etc., with the other participants. While the ceremony does have much in common with the sumble, its origins are actually in the methods used by Brauchers in a Freindschaft when they would gather for their rites.

die **Schaffichheit**: This is the Noble Virtue (see *Reenheide*) of Industriousness. In each lifetime, we are given a unique opportunity to make the most of who we are in the body we are in and with the people who are around us at that time. We are to strive to advance ourselves, our families, our clans, our communities, and, ultimately, all of humanity. We do not advance as a civilization without effort.

die **Scheiding**: The month of September.

der **Scheierschtann**/die **Scheierschtaern**: See *Hexezeeche*.

es **Scheitholt**: Fretted dulcimer, mountain dulcimer, or box zither. The Scheitholt is a traditional Deitsch stringed instrument that is still found in the Deitscherei and in Appalachia today (Marks 14-17).

die **Schillgrott**: Turtle. On the Muunraad, the sixth new moon after Oschdre (the Spring Equinox) is the turtle moon.

die **Schissel**: Bowl. The Schissel is a bowl in which libations are poured throughout an Urglaawe *Sege* or *Sammel*. The bowl serves as a vessel from which the deities may drink of the libation. During Sege, a twig (see *Segezweig*) or a blossom is dipped into the libation and sprinkled upon the participants as a blessing. In Sege and in Sammel, the libation is ultimately poured to the soil or into a stream as an offering to the deities.

die **Schlachtzeit**: Butchering season. This is the time to cull the herds (Tobin, *The Wild Hunt Begins* 9) and to butcher and to prepare meat for consumption over the winter. The season begins at (or around) *Allelieweziel* and, ends when possible, prior to *Yuul* (Shoemaker, *Belsnickel* 34).

A tradition associated with the Schlachtzeit and with Yuul is the gifting of Metzelsupp. It is unknown whether the practice is of Heathen or post-Heathen origin, but the practice is certainly consistent with the gift-for-a-gift concept of Heathenry.

As families completed their butchering, they would create a soup of mixed sausages and meats and send it to their neighbors as a gift. The neighbors who received the soup would, in turn, also make and send Metzelsupp out to their friends and neighbors, including to those who had previously given the soup to them as a gift. The gift exchange often occurred twice in a season, and it was considered highly offensive to receive the soup and not return the gift (Wentz 123-124). Although the soup was initially created from one's own slaughter, in the modern era, adjustments have been made to allow for store-bought meats or for herbal and vegetable soups.

der **Schmaus**: Feast. This is the sacred feast of that takes place during Urglaawe ceremonies. It includes place settings for the honored deities and/or ancestors.

Schneller Geischt: Known in English as a Snallygaster, this legendary, dragon-like creature is known to be a terror in areas of southern Deitscherei, particularly around Braddock Heights, Maryland. Deitsch settlers described Snallygasters as being half-reptile, half-bird, with razor-sharp teeth and a metallic-looking beak. Some descriptions include features such as tentacles, similar to those of an octopus. Like many other serpents or dragons (Gehman 53), Snallygasters are believed to guard treasures.

The Snallygaster has a mortal enemy called a Dwayyo that sounds very similar in description to a *Hexewolf*.

der **Schpeecht**: Woodpecker. On the Muunraad, the fourth new moon after Oschdre (the Spring Equinox) is the woodpecker moon.

der **Schpindelbrauch**: The Spindle Rite is conducted at the beginning of ceremonies honoring goddesses who are closely associated with spinning, particularly Frigg (Gundarsson & Waggoner 39), the *Wurthexe* (Norns) and *Berchta*. The rite would also be relevant for Holle, but the Sichelbrauch is generally used instead.

es **Schpuck**; plural: die **Schpucke**: Spook, ghost. This term refers to haunting spirits as opposed to the more general term *Geischt*.

der **Schtarich**: Stork. The old folk tales of the storks bringing newborns to their parents is not an accurate reflection of the myth, or perhaps it is more accurate to say metaphor, of the stork. Rather than the storks carrying the physical children to the parents, they instead are seen as ferrying the souls of the deceased to their destination with Holle, and, on the opposite end, they are seen to carry the souls that are prepared to be reborn to their points of entry into the bodies of newly formed physical children.

While the metaphor states that the stork picks a child up from a swamp and drops him or her down the chimney (Müller-Ebeling, Rätsch, & Storl 61), it is unlikely that anyone takes that lore literally. The point at which this transfer takes place is still up for debate within a number of Heathen communities. Many believe this transfer takes place immediately upon conception. Others believe it occurs nine days after the birth of the physical form.

der **Schwerpunkt**, der **yaahrzeitlich Schwerpunkt**: Seasonal Focus. Stemming from Braucherei philosophy, the year is cut into eight segments, with the equinoxes and the solstices creating four cardinal points, and four other points, called the cross-quarters, occur in between the cardinals. During each segment, we are to take on a different focus for our individual development. These foci most often relate to achieving progress on New Year's Resolutions.

The Dark Half of Year (see *Dunkelhelft*) begins at *Allelieweziel*.

From Allelieweziel through *Yuul*: The focus is on internal improvement and what could be changed in the next year. At the onset of the New Year (Neiyaahrsdaag), make appropriate resolutions and oaths (see *Eed*).

Neiyaahrsdaag to *Grundsaudaag*: Plan path to goals and procure any needed items.

Grundsaudaag to *Oschdre*: Extinguish old burdens, as symbolized by letting the flame in the hearth burn out and cleaning the hearth on Grundsaudaag.

Oschdre to *Walpurgisnacht*/Moifescht: Put plans into action. Reflect upon the cycle of life, death, and rebirth. Prepare to plant the seeds of change as well as for the seeds of the coming harvest.

The Bright Half of Year (see *Brechthelft*) begins at Moifescht (see *Wonnetdanz*).

Moifescht to *Midsummer*: Experience the joy of life. Resolutions should now be in effect.

Midsummer to *Hoietfescht*: Prepare and store crops and hay. Check progress on resolutions.

Hoietfescht to *Erntfescht*: Recognize the wonders of the universe and the gifts around us. This is a time of celebration and receiving the rewards of hard work.

Erntfescht to Allelieweziel: Reflect upon the Sacred Promise (see *Zusaagpflicht*). By this time, the resolutions should have taken hold and can be ceremonially burned with the *Butzemann*.

die **Seel**: Soul. The soul is an amazingly complex concept in Germanic lore. In seeking a cogent and coherent depiction of the multi-faceted soul of humans, the authors came across many conflicting references in European and Deitsch lore.

Regarding the soul, one thing that all Heathen groups have in common is an understanding that the soul, like the physical body, is composed of multiple parts. The reported number ranges from three to twelve parts. Urglaawer generally conceptualize the soul as having twelve parts. The parts of the physical body do not decay at the same rate after death; neither do the parts of the soul.

Although there are some differences between the Urglaawe and Theodish understanding of the soul, we are indebted to Leon Wild (*The Runes Workbook*) of the Rune Gild and Eric Wodening (*Heathen Soul*) and the Wednesbury Shire of the White Marsh Theod for presenting soul knowledge in a concise format, saving us a significant amount of leg work and analysis.

Geischt: The Geischt is a subset of the Seel. From the Urglaawe perspective, ten parts of the soul constitute the Geischt. They are the portions that relate to the ethereal self. The Leicht relates to the physical self, and the Fetch is able to separate from the other rest of the soul for journeywork. At death, the Fetch may attach itself to other souls.

The portions of the soul that are most likely to be reborn in subsequent generations are the Hoch, Urleeg, and Glick. This does not mean that other portions (or the entirety of the soul) can never be reborn. It simply means that more research must be conducted to understand the mysteries of the soul and the transitions throughout the *Lewesraad*.

Deitsch/Urglaawe Name	Wednesbury Shire	Rune Gild	Interpretation
der *Ochdem*, der *Odem*	Æþem	Athem	The breath of life.
der *Seelhaut*	Hama	Hyde	Takes the shape of the physical body, though some entities can shape-shift. This is the most frequently seen manifestation that we call a ghost (Geischt).

Deitsch/Urglaawe Name	Wednesbury Shire	Rune Gild	Interpretation
der *Hoch*	Hyge	Hugh	The Higher Self. Intellect, analytical capabilities.
der *Megge*	Mægen	**	Spiritual energy that pervades all life. This is the energy that is used for healing in Braucherei.
es *Gemiet*	Mód	Shade (shadow side of self)	The total Self, including one's general disposition or mood.
der *Meind*, der *Sinn*	Mynd	Myne	Memories, ancestral qualities.
es *Urleeg*	Orlæg	**	Primal layer. Individual law. "The hand we are dealt" at birth. Records the actions throughout one's life.
der *Wille*	Willa	**	The force of will. The capability to cause something to occur. Self-determination
die *Gewut*	Wód	Wode	Inspiration. Passions.
es *Glick*	**	Hamingja, Luck	Repository of luck and personal power accumulated throughout one's life.
die *Leich*	Lich	Lyke/Lich	Physical body.
der *Folyer*, die *Folyern*	Fetch, Fæcce	Fetch	Guardian spirit. Journeyer.

** Although some items appear blank in the table, their absence does not indicate that the Rune Gild or the Theods do not integrate those aspects into their lore; it simply means that they do not identify a particular concept as a distinct part of the soul.

For example, Urglaawe and White Marsh Theod both consider Urleeg/Orlæg to be part of the soul. The respective cell in the Rune Gild column is blank. This does not mean that Wild and the Rune Gild do not share the concept of Urleeg or have their own perspectives regarding it. It merely means that they do not incorporate Urleeg as a specific, distinct, component of the soul.

der **Seelhaut**: The "soul skin." See *Seel*.

der **Sege**: Blessing, faining. This is the equivalent of the blòt (*Blutvergiesse)* or the fain (*Fagge)* in other Heathen traditions. In Urglaawe, the Sege is the most commonly held ceremonial exchange of gifts with the deities.

die **Segezweig**: Blessing twig. A Segezweig is used to sprinkle the participants with blessed libation from a *Sege*. The Segezweig may also be used to draw a rune on the forehead of the participants with the libation instead of sprinkling.

der **Seidel**: Stein, tankard. Due to cultural context, a Seidel is more commonly used in Urglaawe rituals than is a drinking horn (*Drinkhann*). However, either may be used.

der **Seider**: Apple cider, which is commonly used in Urglaawe rituals as a non-alcoholic alternative to the more typical alcoholic libations (see *Drankopfer*).

der **Selbschtreiguck**: This is the ancillary virtue (see *Reenheide*) of Introspection, which is emphasized most strongly during the season between *Allelieweziel* and *Yuul* (see *Schwerpunkt*). Introspection leads to the illumination of the self, which leads to spiritual growth and change.

die **Selbschtverbessering**: The ancillary virtue (see *Reenheide*) of Self-Improvement. Our lives improve when we make an effort to improve them. This is the purpose behind the New Year's Resolution (see *Vorsatz*).

es **Selbschtzuverdraue**: This is the Noble Virtue (see *Reenheide*) of Self-Reliance. Relying on our own strength, wit, and resolve is the best way for us to create a free community and to advance human consciousness.

die **Sichel**: Sickle. See *Hollesichel*.

der **Sichelbrauch**: The Sickle Rite. This incantation opens many ceremonies that are sacred to the goddess, Holle. It typically involves the holding of a physical sickle. The sickle is used to close ceremonies by symbolically cutting the activity.

die **Sippschaft**: A Sippschaft is an Urglaawe kindred with oaths.

der **Stav**, der **Schtaab**: Stav. Stav is a martial art passed down through the Hafskjold family of Norway. Most aspects of Heathenry take into account the expansion of spirital, social, and mental consciousness. While Braucherei and other living traditions take into account the healing and the blessing of the physical body, Stav takes the physical aspects further. Stav presents a discipline of runic stances that make the *Megge* (main; life force) flow through the body. It also uses the runic stances for posturing and maneuvering in a martial arts context. For more information on Stav in the United States, see the website of Ice & Fire at http://www.iceandfire.us.

der **Straussdanz**: Strouse Dance. This is an unusual piece of "Deitschiana," which is currently undergoing a small revival. Strouse Dances were social events that involved the winning of prizes (mostly female attire) and included socializing, music, and dancing. The dance reference comes from the practice of attaching a lit candle and a key to a string. While the candle burned, the participants danced in a circle around the flame. When the candle burned the string and fell to the floor, whoever held the key won the prize (Yoder *Strouse* 15-16). Despite many churches looking askance at these social occasions as being witches dances, they were popular enough to be reported in various areas of the Deitscherei.

Teitonisch (adjective): Teutonic. This term is used to include all Scandinavian and Germanic peoples.

die **Teutoburgschlacht**: The Battle of Teutoburg Forest occured on September 9 in the year 9, CE. A German tribal alliance led by Arminius destroyed three Roman legions, which were under the command of Publius Quinctilius Varus. This is one of very few Germanic combat victories over the Roman military.

die **Treie**: This is the Noble Virtue (see *Reenheide*) of Troth or Fidelity. Dependability and loyalty to our faith and values is of the utmost importance. This concept includes diligence in our work and in our duties.

We also must ensure that we are engaging in activities and projects for the right reasons. Partaking in endeavors for the wrong purposes corrupts the work and results in a potential for unexpected consequences.

Braucherei provides examples of this corruption even in gift giving. If negative thoughts are on the mind of the giver, then the negativity can be transferred to the gift, thus tainting the gift and perhaps even making the gift detrimental to the recipient. In this case, it would be better for the giver not to send a gift at all. If the gift is in response to a gift given, it is better for the giver to wait until he is in a better state of mind or to send a gift without personal contact (via a third party).

der **Tuisto**: Also known as Tuisco. Tacitus reports in *Germania* that the Germans worshiped the earth-sprung god, Tuisto, through old songs. While, on the surface the name Tuisto seems to have some etymologic relationship with *Ziu*, the description of Him as being "earth-sprung" could lead one to consider the possibility that Tuisto is of the *Wane* and is thus not the same god as Ziu.

The possibility of Tuisto being of the Wane is supported by Tacitus' claim that Tuisto is the father of Mannus, who, in turn, fathered the Ingvaeones, Istvaeones, and the Irminones. The name of the Ingvaeones translates to "people of Yngvi" or "people of Ing," with Ing being another name for the Wane god Frey.

Grimm suggests that Tuisto may have been hermaphroditic and may even be the same entity as the Norse Ymir. Unlike Ymir, though, Tuisto was celebrated and honored. Grimm also draws connections to the post-Vedic Hindu Tvastar.

It is currently impossible to prove or to disprove Tacitus' claims or Grimm's theories. However, the personal experiences of some Urglaawer describe Tuisto as a Wan and suggest an association between Him and *Ewicher Yeeger*.

der **Turmlutzer**: Tower lantern. This lantern holds two candles: one on the outside on the top and the other inside an inner chamber. The location of the candles reflects the strength of the goddess Sunna's touch upon the Earth in a given season. At *Midsummer*, the candle on the top burns brightly. At *Yuul*, the candle burns in the inner chamber and is extinguished at the beginning of the Yuul Sege. It is lit again in order to represent the victory of light over darkness.

Other Germanic groups, particularly the Irminen, use similar lanterns with variations on the candle presentation (Coulter 227).

die **Ufffassing**: Thew; order. This is a term for the conceptualization and the interpretation of the *Ordning* and other aspects of the social and moral codes of a Sippschaft.

die **Uffwaarting**: This is the Noble Virtue (see *Reenheide*) of Hospitality. Being a good host is ordained by the Norse *Hávamál*, or the Words of the High One, which is attributed to Odin (*Wodan*). Hospitality helps to create goodwill among members of a community, and, in conjunction with other virtues, can help to thwart the "rootlessness" and loneliness that plagues modern society.

der **Urboge**: The shortest path of the sun in the sky, occurring close to the winter solstice (Winkler, *Pennsylvania German Astronomy and Astrology V*, 38).

der **Urglaawe**: Literally "primal faith." Urglaawe is the name of a Heathen path that is derived from the living, pre-Christian traditions of the Deitsch nation.

der **Urglaawer** (male); die **Urglaawern** or **Urglaawerin** (female); die **Urglaawer** (plural): An adherent to the Urglaawe path or sect of Heathenry.

es **Urleeg**: The primal layers known as Ørlög in Scandinavian lore. This concept is similar to (and related to) Wyrd (see *Wurt*). Many aspects of our identity, individuality, and construction are hereditary. Urleeg is a part of the soul (*Seel*) that is present at the time of birth and records our actions into our Wurt. The state of Urleeg in the current life will heavily influence the state of our souls in thenext life. Thus, our actions in one life can have a very strong influence on the quality of our next life. See also *Seel*.

Vatni Ausa: See *Daaf.*

die **Verwalting**: Verwalting is the ancillary virtue (see *Reenheide*) of Stewardship. Careful management of resources and the world around us is a core component of Urglaawe, of Braucherei, and of the traditional Deitsch culture. Akin to the Noble Virtues of Discipline (see *Addning*) and Hospitality (*Uffwarting*), Verwalting helps to create a stable living environment for all of creation.

Stewardship does not mean a lack of progress, an austere lifestyle, or a restricted diet. It does, though, indicate that progress must not be reckless, that creatures must not be hunted to extinction, and that resources must not be squandered in order to achieve immediate goals. It is nearly impossible to live on Earth and not have a negative impact upon or alter one's environment. However, we can strive to minimize the impact, to correct or to ameliorate damages done previously, and to improve our circumstances going forward.

This aspect of Deitsch culture does not emanate from post-modern jargon. The virtue of Stewardship is closely associated with the *Zusaagpflicht* or the Sacred Duty.

All of Heathenry, including Urglaawe, still constitutes only a small segment of society. However, small rocks can create a big wake by making a splash. The most effective way of making change is to lead by example. Stewardship includes being conscious of the world around us. We are to take care of the land and to treat the life around you (including humans!) with respect. When possible, we are to know what we are eating and where it comes from (admittedly a difficult task!). Verwalting tells us to develop and to utilize our resources with deliberation and a view of the future, and, to the extent of your personal inclination, act politically for appropriate change.

The Deitsch culture, up until very recently, was very geared towards the stewardship of the land and of resources. In most places, it still is. However, a mindless consumer culture is creeping in, and, with its promises of gratification, it is a threat to the Stewardship culture of this region.

die **Verwandschaft**: The ancillary virtue (see *Reenheide*) of Kinship reflects the need that all of us have to belong to a community. Despite the efforts of the consumer culture to separate and divide people in order to increase corporate bottom lines, it is unnatural for humans not to live and to exist in a social setting. Kinship, along with other virtues, can help to create an environment of security, trust, and interdependence among the members of a community. Even while we embrace Self-Reliance (see *Selbschtzuverdraue*), we also embrace that community interdependence, which is reflected in the Heathen concepts of gift exchanges (see *Edelmut*) and frith (see *Fruchsfriede*).

der **Voll**: God of the *Ase*. See *Phol*.

die **Volla**: Known in Scandinavian lore as Fulla (Simek 96). She is a goddess of the *Ase* who is associated with abundance and wealth. She appears in the Second Merseburg Charm (see *Merseburg Incantations*). Based on the text of the Second Merseburg Charm, She is the sister of *Frigg*. See also *Phol*.

der **Vorsatz**; plural: **Vorsetz**: Resolutions or promises, such as those made on New Year's Day. See *Schwerpunkt*.

die **Waahr**, die **Waahra**: Goddess known as Vár from sources, including the *Þrymskviða*, or *Thrym's Poem* in the *Poetic Edda* (Larrington 101). In Urglaawe, She witnesses oaths, contracts, and vows, including marital vows.

die **Waahretsaagerei**: Divination. While runes (see *Roon*) are the most common tools of divination in Urlgaawe, many other tools have also been used into the present era. Among the many, varied items listed for divination uses are diapers (Dieffenbach 23), bees (Breininger 38), goose bones (reported within the Oley Freindschaft), dowsing (Shoemaker *Water* 25-27), and a long history of astrological practice and interpretation (Winkler).

While some of these practices, most notably many aspects of the astrology, were not of Germanic origin, the relationship to the Germanic culture and climate influenced the interpretation of the astrological readings, predictions, and agricultural lore.

See also *Muunraad*.

die **Waahrheit**: The Noble Virtue of Truth includes recognizing existence as it really is. We have the power, and the obligation, to shape our reality, but first we have to confront the circumstances as they are now. Basing our existence, interactions, and interdependence on Truth helps to ensure strong bonds within a family, clan, or community.

die **Waerrickgawwel**: Distaff, spindle. The distaff and/or the spindle is sacred to numerous goddesses but is most closely identified with *Frigg*. Along with the hammer (*Dunner*), sickle (*Holle*), helmet or glove (*Ziu*), the spindle is one of the primary tools used to hallow an altar.

die **Waertunge**: Values; thew. This term relates to the values that are held by a Sippschaft, Freibesitz, or any community.

die **Walkyrie**: Valkyrie. Much is known of these semi-divine female beings from Scandinavian lore. However, even given the knowledge therein, much about these entities remains a mystery. Because most Urglaawer do not ascribe, at least not wholly, to the concept of the slain being taken to Valhalla (the hall of Odin) and Sessrumnir (the hall of Freya), we will look at other theories.

Generally, the perception in Urglaawe is that seeing a Walkyrie is a portent of doom, death, or destruction. She does not necessarily bring about the destructive events, however. Some theories present the Walkyrie as a "guardian angel" type of being (Grimm 418), while other theories view them as "soul hunters," who grab the souls of the dead (all dead, not just those slain in battle) and present them to the appropriate deity before beginning the process of rebirth (see *Widdergeburt*).

Yet another theory states that the Walkyrie are similar in function to the *Elbekeenich* or to the Irish Banshee, appearing soon before death.

It should be noted, though, that the meaning of the term "Valkyrie" means "chooser of the battle-slain," so the terminology supports the Scandinavian view. Some theories surrounding the terminology point to a possibility that the Walkyrie would be Shield Maidens or Idis (Simek 349) known by other names or placed into other roles.

die **Wane** (plural term); der **Wan** (sing. masc); die **Wanin** (sing. fem.): The tribe of deities known to the Scandinavians as the

Vanir. These deities are generally associated with the rhythms and cycles of nature. Among the most well known of the Wane, we find *Holle, Berchta, Frey, Freya,* Nadd (known as *Njörðr* in Scandinavian lore), *Tuisto*, and *Ewicher Yeeger*. See also *Ase*.

die **Walpurgisnacht**: *Holle*, being known in the syncretic era and being taken into the post-conversion era as Walburga, returns to the physical plane form the Wild Hunt, and the time of fertile fields draws near. On the current calendar, this would be the night of April 30. However, since Heathen days begin at dusk, the night of April 30 on the secular calendar would be the night of 1. Wonnet (May 1) on the spiritual calendar.

The Dark Half of the Year ends on this night, and the parade of Wights returning behind Holle is reflected in this last event that involves costumes and masks. Deitsch tradition holds that Spring Cleaning is to be completed by this date, and doors and windows are to be opened with a written greeting placed on them (Tobin, *May Day!* 3) welcoming Holle to come to inspect the house. Order will be rewarded; disorder may require explanation.

See also *Wonnetdanz*.

die **Wasserschpritz**: See *Daaf.*

die **Weisheit**: The ancillary virtue (see *Reenheide*) of Wisdom. Without the wisdom to understand the world around us, to interpret what events mean to us, and to act appropriately in response to stimuli, the successful application of the other virtues is highly unlikely.

die **Weisskeppich Fraa,** also known as **Weisskeppichi Fraa**: White-Haired Woman. An Urglaawe goddess known uniquely through Braucherei. She is referred to as the first practitioner of Braucherei (Tobin, *Powwow Birds* 7) and is sometimes compared to the Norse Eir.

Descriptions of this goddess allow for a link between Her and the White Ladies (Grimm, pp. 962-968). Some theories propose that Weisskeppichi Fraa is Berchta. These theories emerge from the fact that the Goldeneil, or golden owl, is sacred to Her (Tobin, *Powwow Birds* 7) and the owl (see *Eil*) is sacred to Berchta, and also because Berchta's name means "white" (Grimm, 968).

However, there is insufficient supporting evidence for this claim. Weisskeppichi Fraa frequently appears alongside Holle, thus negating theories that Holle and She are one and the same. Therefore, Die Weisskeppich Fraa is, most likely, a White Lady whose name either is lost to time or is awaiting our discovery within the Braucher interviews that still need to be catalogued.

Die Weisskeppich Fraa is known to be the paramount of healing -- physically, mentally, and spiritually.

die **Wicht**; die **Wichde** (plural): Wight. These include any number of land spirits, home spirits, water spirits, etc. Some, such as the Wassernix on the Wyomissing Creek, are known in oral lore. Some are sympathetic to humans, while some are antipathetic or indifferent. Some antipathetic spirits will respond favorably to respect and/or gifts. The success or failure of a homestead can depend on the relationship built with the wights, the plant spirits, and the animal spirits of the land.

die **Widdergeburt**: Rebirth. Most Urglaawer believe that an immortal portion of the human soul, specifically the Higher Self (Hoherer Selbscht), is reborn into subsequent generations, usually along bloodlines. Some theories include that, during the soul's processing, they are commended into Hel's possession until a suitable incarnation arises, and then Holle returns the soul to this plane. Not all souls are destined for rebirth, however. The souls of some individuals become *Idis*. Other souls may be rendered to the hall of a patron or patroness deity for some time prior to rebirth.

Wildi Yacht: The Wild Hunt or the Furious Host. From the Urglaawe perspective, the Wild Hunt begins on *Allelieweziel* (October 31). Holle leads the Hunt (Chisholm 74) for the souls of the lost or the recently departed. The onset of the Wild Hunt begins a new spiritual year and the Dark Half of the Year (see *Dunkelhelft*).

Depictions of the Wild Hunt take place in the form of costumes or parades, starting with tricks-or-treats (not a customary Deitsch event but it has become part of the culture). Next is Der Reifkeenich (King Frost) in November. Although the King Frost Carnival in Hamburg, PA, was only created in 1910 (Jordan 130-

131), a tradition of railing against the coming frost is known in Braucherei in Carbon County.

"Belsnickeling" in December prior to Yule was the original time of tricks-or-treats in the Deitscherei (see *Wodan, Yuul*).

Mummenschanz (a remnant of which is the Mummer's Parade in Philadelphia) originated in the Swedish section of the city but was also part of the Deitsch celebrations (Jordan 128).

The Carnivals of Europe and Mardi Gras of New Orleans very likely have their roots in depictions of the Wild Hunt. These depictions may also be combined with efforts of the folk to beat back winter. See *Fasching*.

April Fool may well be remnants of Heathen practices in England.

The final event is *Walpurgisnacht*, which in modern times in parts of Germany and Austria is an event full of costumes and masks.

der **Wille**: Will; intent. This is the aspect of one's personality and the portion of one's soul (see *Seel*) that provides the ability for self-determination an to bring about change in the world. Using one's Wille is the very basis of magic, including *Braucherei* and *Hexerei*.

der **Winsch**: Although "Winsch" is a byname of *Wodan*, in this entry, we are referring to the New Year's wishes that revelers and visitors traditionally conduct in various areas of the Deitscherei. The wishes are often long and verbose, but they are intended to start the year off well. The wishers are usually rewarded with food or drink (Haag 108-113; Stoudt 102-117).

der **Wodan**, der **Wudan**: Wotan, Odin. As is the case with most other Heathen paths, He is seen in Urglaawe as the All-Father and the Seeker, and He is credited with providing the breath of life to humanity and with bringing forth the awareness of the runes. Despite post-conversion attempts to link Santa Claus to Saint Nicholas, Wodan, particularly His aspect of Wish-Granter, is the true inspiration behind the "jolly old elf" (Shoemaker, *Belsnickel* 34).

Within Deitsch culture, though, there is another character, who is a manifestation of Wodan: der Belsnickel. Shoemaker and Yoder (79) report that Belsnickel was seen as a precursor to St. Nicholas and Santa Claus. While the name "Belsnickel" means "Nicholas in pelts," the links to St. Nicholas are again contrived. Der Belsnickel is, again, Wodan in a disguise as Wanderer and Seeker of Wisdom.

The human depiction of Belsnickel typically consists of a man dressed in pelts going from door to door across the neighborhood. He asks riddles, sometimes complicated and esoteric, of children and adults alike. Acceptable answers are rewarded with a gift of chestnuts (Shoemaker, *Belsnickel* 37). Unacceptable answers result in the respondent having to attempt to grab a chestnut while trying to avoid having a hickory or willow switch strike his/her hand. Interestingly, there are indicators in Deitsch culture that chestnuts are sacred to Wodan, which again draws a link between Belsnickel and Wodan.

die **Wonnet**: The month of May.

der **Wonnetdanz**: On Wonnet/May 1, we hold the dance of joy, or the Moifescht, as a festival of Holle. Holle has returned from the Wild Hunt during the night (see *Walpurgisnacht*). A celebration of male creative energies is found in the constructing and decorating of the Maypole or Queschtbaam. Christian descriptions of Walpurgisnacht and the Wonnetdanz are full of fear of "witches" and the destruction that the dance does to the fields upon which they took place (Jordan 216).

die **Wurt**: Wurt is the Deitsch term for the force of Wyrd, which is a concept seen most clearly in Anglo-Saxon Heathenry that compares roughly to a fate or destiny. However, the future is not set, and while it is possible to predict likely outcomes based on the present, one may alter his or her Wurt through actions and deeds. All living things, including the deities, are subject to Wurt. The actions of one's life eventually become recorded in one's *Urleeg* and are transmitted into the next life.

Some Urglaawer see Wurt as an aspect of a supreme creative life force, bringing matter into existence and carrying it through the cycles and spirals of life, death, and rebirth. Whether such a creative life force exists and is personal, impersonal, conscious, or unconscious is still a matter of debate.

die **Wurthexe**: The Three Sisters, also known as the Norns and the Weird (Wyrd) Sisters, are seen as weaving the fabric of *Wurt* for all living beings in creation. The three Norns known in Scandinavian lore are Urðr, Verðandi, and Skuld, but there are also other Norns, who descend from the deities, from the elves, and from the dwarves (Simek 236-237). The Urglaawe concept of the Wurthexe is very similar to that of the three best-known Norns. One represents the past, one the present, and one the most likely future. While *Frigg* spins the fabric, the Wurthexe arrange the strands according to one's *Urleeg* and actions of the past and present.

Some theories suggest that the Wurthexe may be akin to the Matres and Matrones, who were female deities honored on votives in North and West Europe. Over 1100 inscriptions are known (Simek 204), about half of which present Germanic names. The topics of the Wurthexe and of the Matres and Matrones are still in need of more research and philosophical organization.

der **Yuul**: Yule, beginning at sunset on December 20 and carrying through Twelfth Night on December 31 (*Berchtaslaaf*), ending on January 1 (Feast of *Frey*).

It is fairly common knowledge that American secular Christmas practices stem principally from Deitsch and Netherlands Dutch customs, particularly since the Puritans did not celebrate the holiday (Shoemaker & Yoder xiii). The colors of red and green stem from plants such as holly, which are associated with Heathen Yule.

The presence of the reindeer has a decidedly "Northern" feel to it, particularly since reindeer are not native to the region where Saint Nicholas lived. Braucherei lore tells us that the primary individuals in the sleigh are *Wodan* (Santa Claus) and Holle ("Mrs. Claus"). The other characters along with them (Knecht Rubrecht, Schwatzer Piet, etc.) are depictions of the spirits who are accompanying the deities on the Wild Hunt.

Although Urglaawe views Holle as the leader of the Wild Hunt, Wodan is also a participant in the fury. However, there is a slight dissonance between Santa Claus being the primary entity in the sleigh and Holle leading the Wild Hunt. One possible reason for the lack of symmetry is that the Yule "sleigh" scenario originated among a different contributing Teutonic tribe than did the Wild Hunt concepts. However, this theory is, at this time, merely conjecture. More research on this topic is required.

Another depiction of the Wild Hunt appears during the Yuletide: Belsnickeling. This practice is somewhat similar to the tricks-or-treats that one finds at Halloween. People dress up in costumes, parade through the streets, and stop at homes to receive fruit or candy. This tradition continues in Deitsch areas of central (Winey 10-13), northern Pennsylvania, West Virginia, and Virginia (Milnes 185-188). Unfortunately, over the last three decades, it has been lost in much of the Deitscherei due to Halloween's prominence. Efforts to revive the tradition in the Deitscherei have had some success.

See also *Wodan*.

die **Yuuling**: The month of December.

der **Zauber**: A spell, spoken charm, or an incantation. See also *Bann, banne*.

der **Zauberer** (male); die **Zaubererin** or **Zauberern** (female): A magician. This is a general term and does not connote either Braucherei or Hexerei.

die **Zauberei**: Magic. Zauberei is any form of magic, especially magic involving increasing something (power, wealth, health) or exerting influence. See also *Bannerei, banne*.

der **Zauberzettel**: Charm ticket. The Zauberzettel is a written charm on a small piece of paper. It is used as a talisman or a block to protect against negative energy. It is commonly used in house blessings (see *Haussege*), where it is tucked away in windowsills, doors, chimney flues, and any other openings to the outside. It is never to be affixed with any metal, such as a paper clip.

die **Zeitschnur**, es **Zeitschnurwaerrick**: Referred to in English as time-cord work, this is a form of journeying that seems to be unique to the Deitsch. The imagery used includes a web formed by the umbilical cords of ancestors and descendants. All time- or family-related aspects of Braucherei and Urglaawe include the future and subsequent generations as well as the past and the forebears. One major caveat in dealing with the descendants, though, is that the future is not set in stone.

The descendants who appear in time-cord work are those who are most likely to exist in the future given the circumstances of the present. Thus, a given descendant appearing in one instance of time-cord work might not appear in a subsequent journey. Such a shift can be somewhat disorienting and very stressful. While potential descendants can offer amazing insights into the events that occurred in their past -- our present or future -- care should be taken to ensure proper preparation for the risks involved in dealing with descendants who may never come to be.

der **Zieb** (male); die **Ziebin** (female); die **Ziewe** (plural): God, Goddess, Deities. The term is a neologism from "*Ziu*," which is the name of Tyr in Deitsch. The root of "Ziu" meant "god" in Old High German. The deities are seen as our elder kin. They are distinct individuals with their own personalities, strengths, and weaknesses. They are not generally seen as immortal; they are sustained by Idunn's apples (see *Abbel*). They can be killed and injured, and most of them will perish at the end of this cosmic cycle (see *Gedderdemmerung*).

der **Ziewer** (male); die **Ziewerin** or **Ziewern** (female); die **Ziewer** (plural): One who serves the deities; godsman or godswoman. See also *Diener*.

die **Zing**: This is a spoken word that is often repeated as part of a Braucherei charm (see *Zauber*, *Zauberei*). It has the impact of weakening the targeted affliction. The word very likely comes from "zieh dei Gift" or "draw thy poison" (Hertzog 24).

die **Zisa**: Zisa is seen as the founder and protector of the city of Augsburg in modern Bavaria. Augsburg was known earlier as Zizarim. Zisa was reported under various names (including Isis due to language confusion, apparently). She was particularly associated with the Suevi, who are predecessors of the Swabians. The Suevi also mixed with the Alemanni and other tribes. There are quite a few locations in southern Germany and Switzerland named for Her. The tribes who knew Her were large contributors to the Pennsylvania German nation.

In the first century BCE, the Romans under Titus Annius laid siege to Zizarim just before Her feast day. Unfortunately for the Romans, many Swabian warriors were coming to Zizarim for the festival, and on Her day they attacked the Romans and throttled them (Pennick 107).

Granted, the Romans years later did take the city, but the battle for Zizarim was a famous loss for Rome. Despite the loss of the city and the subsequent Christian suppression, Her presence remained.

Zisa in the Christian era was depicted as the Virgin Mary with the extra appellation of "Undoer-of-Knots." Images of Her from later centuries indicate that she has the ability to remove obstacles or, some believe, even to undo Urleeg if one's cause is just. Images of Her in this role have been restored in Augsburg's city hall, though they were from later centuries originally (Pennick 108).

She was so widely revered among the Suevi that their dialects called Tuesday "Zistag" not after Ziu but after Her. The Diocese of Augsburg banned the name Zistag and called it "Aftermontag" (After-Monday; Pennick 109).

There are quite a few places that bear her name as the root of their modern names. The church of St. Peter am Perlach stands on the grounds of Her temple at Zisenberg in Augsburg.

Her symbol is the pinecone and appears in Augsburg even in some churches (Pennick 109). As the pinecone protects the seeds, so does She protect her people. The pinecone symbolizes protection, regeneration, and continuity. Even though the Romans eventually conquered Augsburg, the Volk's relationship to Zisa continued, in symbolic form if not conscious form, into the present day.

The pinecone even now appears on the coat of arms of Augsburg (see image below).

...asege: Ceremony honoring the goddess *Zisa* on Her feast ...ich is 28. Scheiding or September 28.

der **Ziu**: Tyr, Tiw. Ziu was the early Sky God and, very likely, the original chief of the Aesir. His name is carried in English within the word "Tuesday." In German, the name of the day is "Dienstag," which implies an element of service. In Deitsch, the name is "Dinschdaag," which is clearly related to "Dienstag," but we are fortunate enough to have the term resemble the word "Ding," (see *Ding*), for which Ziu is frequently the overseer. Items in Urglaawe that are considered sacred to Ziu include gloves, spears, aconite (Tyr's Helm), the North Star, and the Tiwaz rune.

die **Zusaagpflicht**, die **Zusaagfassing**: The closest loose translation would be that of a "Sacred Duty" or a "Sacred Promise" as it relates to an unspoken moral and ethical "contract" among the plant, animal, human, mineral, and spirit realms (Tobin, *The Sacred Promise* 14, 16). This concept of symbioses comes straight from Braucherei and relates to stewardship (see *Verwalting*) and conscious living of the world around us. While it is not certain that the terminologies or the organized concepts behind them are of Heathen-era origin, they are almost certainly evolved from a Heathen worldview of personal responsibility and self-discipline (see *Addning*).

Even though no one really knows how old this concept is, it is certainly consistent with Heathen worldviews. As part of a living culture, though, it has evolved within Deitsch culture (and presumably Palatinate, Swabian, Westphalian, Hessian, Silesian, Alsatian, and Swiss cultures prior to emigration) over the centuries.

Each domain (humanity, plants, and animals) has had, since time immemorial, roles to perform in the cycle of life (*Lewesraad*). The roles evolved over the course of time and developed into an unwritten or spiritual social contract (to use Hobbesian terminology).

Our modern society separates us not only from the reality of the seasons but also from the plant and animal kingdoms. Although we are fortunate enough to live close to the land here in this area, much of our food is still processed and appears as convenient little meals. An understanding of the Sacred Duty includes recognizing and respecting the loss of life, whether animal or vegetable, that resulted in those meals.

Recently, there have been efforts here in parts of Pennsylvania to reduce sludge farming (the disposal of wastewater on farmlands), to put an end to the inhumane treatment of puppy mills, and to end some of the more destructive practices of Big Agro that have resulted in a great volume of food but, very likely, in less actual nutrition. These efforts are all aiming to put an end to violations of the Sacred Promise.

As almost any good, effective manager knows, being at the top of an organization does not mean that power can be used indiscriminately. Eventually, morale breaks down among the staff. Rancor develops, and the health of the organization grows sour. The same arrangement exists throughout the physical world. The fact that mankind <u>can</u> do something does not mean he <u>should</u> do it. Morale is breaking down throughout the physical world as a result of the abuses therein. In a manner of M. Night Shyamalan's *The Happening* (which was filmed not far in Pennsylvania from where this book was written, actually), the land may someday rebel or simply to die off.

Living consciously and deliberately within the parameters of the Zusaagpflicht can also help to diminish the impact on our Wyrd (*Wurt*) that we draw simply from the need to eat in order to survive. The Zusaagpflicht is not a call to perfection or austerity. It is, however, a matter of maximizing respect for, and harmony with, the creation and life around us.

der **Zwarich**: Equivalent of the Dwarf. While the Scandinavians generally considered Dwarves to be a subset of Elves (Simek 68), Urglaawe views the two as distinct races. When manifesting themselves in visible form, Dwarves are shorter than humans and are somewhat irascible. The Scandinavian reports of Dwarves' skill as craftsmen match folk tales regarding them as underground miners and metalworkers.

Akin to the Zwarich are earth spirits (Erdgeischt) known in English as gnomes.

der **Zweck**: Purpose. The discussion of the purpose of a ceremony typically precedes the Sege. The discussion helps to create an understanding of the ceremony and also allows for the transmission of oral and written lore.

die **Zweig**: Twig. See *Segezweig*.

Zwelfdi Nacht: Twelfth Night, December 31 into January 1. This is the night of the *Berchtaslaaf*.

Bibliography

Adams, Charles J., III. *Ghost Stories of Berks County, Book 2.* Reading, PA: Exeter House Books, 2002.

Adams, Charles J., III. *Haunted Berks County.* Reading, PA: Exeter House Books, 2005.

Aswynn, Freya. *Northern Mysteries & Magick.* Woodbury, MN: Llewellyn Publications, 2010.

Aswynn, Freya. *Power and Principles of the Runes.* Loughborough, UK: Thoth Publications, 2007.

Aurand, A. Monroe, Jr. *Popular Home Remedies and Supersititions of the Pennsylvania German.* Harrisburg: The Aurand Press, ND.

Barrick, Mac E. *German-American Folklore.* Little Rock: August House, 1987.

Barrick, Mac E. "Moon-Signs in Cumberland County." *Pennsylvania Folklife* vol. 15 no. 4 pp. 41-43. Lancaster, PA: Pennsylvania Folklore Society, Summer 1966.

Beam, C. Richard, ed. *The Thomas R. Brendle Collection of Pennsylvania German Folklore.* Schaefferstown, PA: Historic Schaefferstown, 1995.

Behringer, Wolfgang. *Shaman of Oberstdorf.* Charlottesville: University of Virginia Press, 1994.

Bernario, Herbert W. *Tacitus: Agricola, Germany, and Dialogue on Orators.* Indianapolis: Hackett Publishing Company, Inc., 2006. ISBN: 0-87220-812-5.

Boyer, Dennis. *Once Upon a Hex.* Oregon, Wisconsin: Badger Books, 2004.

Boyer, Dennis. "Soul Work on Halloween." *Hollerbeier Haven* vol. 1 no. 3, pp. 2-3. Kempton, PA: Three Sisters Center for the Healing Arts, November 2007.

Breininger, Lester. "Beekeeping and Bee Lore in Pennsylvania." *Pennsylvania Folklife* v. 16 no. 1, Autumn 1966. Lancaster, PA: Pennsylvania Folklife Society.

Brendle, Thomas R. and Claude W. Unger. "Folk Medicine of the Pennsylvania Germans: The Non-Occult Cures." *Proceedings of the Pennsylvania German Society* 45. Norristown, PA, 1935.

Brendle, Thomas R. and Claude W. Unger. "Witchcraft in Cow and Horse." *The Pennsylvania Dutchman* v. 8 no. 1, Summer 1956. Bethel, PA: The Pennsylvania Dutch Folklore Center, pp. 28-31.

Brown, Frank. "New Light on 'Mountain Mary.'" *Pennsylvania Folklife*, vol. 15, no. 3, pp. 10-15. Lancaster, PA: Pennsylvania Folklife Society, Spring 1966.

Burger, Simone. "Pennsylvania German and the Public Schools." *Der Reggebogge*, 29/1995/1, 21-28, doi: 1995.

Byock, Jesse, trans. *The Prose Edda*. New York: Penguin Group, 2005.

Chisholm, James. *Grove and Gallows*. Smithville, TX: Runa-Raven Press, 2002.

Clubb, Orva Gaile, 2009. *Frau Holda's Tale*. "Hollerbeier Haven: Journal of Traditional Deitsch Wisdom," pp 3-4, 10-13. Autumn 2009. Kempton, PA: Three Sisters Center.

Coulter, James Hjuka. *Germanic Heathenry: A Practical Guide*. Fairfield, CA: 1st Book Publishing, 2003.

Davidson, H.R. *Gods and Myths of Northern Europe*. London: Penguin Books, 1965.

Devlin, Ron. "Early Pike Township Folk Healer Remembered. *Reading Eagle*, November 9, 2009. Accessed March 11, 2012 on the Reading Eagle website: http://readingeagle.com/article.aspx?id=165072

Dickerson, Cody. "Weißt Du zu Ritzen?" *Hex Magazine*, issue 1, pp. 36-40. Portland, OR: Hex Press, Spring & Summer 2007.

Donmoyer, Patrick. "Blumme-Schterne: Flower Stars." *Hollerbeier Haven* v. 2 no. 2, p. 17. Kempton, PA: The Three Sisters Center for the Healing Arts, Fall 2008.

Donmoyer, Patrick. "Hagal - The Holy Hail." *Hollerbeier Haven* v. 4 no. 1, pp. 9-10. Kempton, PA: The Three Sisters Center for the Healilng Arts, Summer 2010.

Dieffenbach, Victor. "Diaper Lore." *The Pennsylvania Dutchman*, v. 8 no. 1, Summer 1956. Kutztown, PA: Craftsmen, Inc.

Drachman, Albert I. and Marian Winston. "Tracking the Elusive Distelfink." *The Dutchman*, vol. 6, no. 5, pp. 28-35. Lancaster, PA: Pennsylvania Dutch Folklore Center, Summer 1955.

Fogel, Edwin Miller, Ph.D. *Beliefs and Superstitions of the Pennsylvania Germans*. Millersville, PA: Center for Pennsylvania German Studies, 1995.

Fogel, Edwin Miller, Ph.D. *Proverbs of the Pennsylvania Germans*. Millersville, PA: Center for Pennsylvania German Studies, 1995.

Frey, J. William. "Des Bucklich Mennli." *The Pennsylvania Dutchman*, vol. 1, no. 22, p. 8. Lancaster, PA: The Pennsylvania Dutch Folklife Center, January, 1950.

Friesen, John W. "The Myth of the Ideal Folk Society versus the Reality of Amish Life." *Pennsylvania Folklife* vol. 43, no. 3, pp. 136-144. Collegeville, PA: Pennsylvania Folklife Society, Spring 1994.

Friesen, Steve. "Home is Where the Hearth Is." *Pennsylvania Folklife* v. 40, no. 3, pp. 98-118. Collegeville, PA: Pennsylvania Folklife Society, Spring 1991.

Gehman, Henry S. "Ghost Stories and Old Superstitions of Lancaster County." *Pennsylvania Folklife* vol. 19, no. 4, pp. 48-53. Lancaster, PA: Pennsylvania Folklife Society, Summer 1970.

Gibbons, Phebe Earle. *Pennsylvania Dutch & Other Essays*. Mechanicsburg, PA: Stackpole Books, 2001.

Graeff, Arthur D. and George M. Meiser, IX. *Echoes of Scholla—Illustrated*. Kutztown, PA: The Berksiana Foundation, 1976.

Graeff, Marie. "Folk Songs." *Pennsylvania Folklife* vol. 31 no. 1, pp. 20-25. Collegeville, PA: Pennsylvania Folklife Society, Autumn 1981.

Grimm, Jacob, James Stallybrass, trans. *Teutonic Mythology* (4 vols). New York: Dover Publications, 1966.

Grönbech, Vilhelm. *Culture of the Teutons*. London: Oxford University Press, 1931.

Guerber, H. A., Shawn Conners, ed. *Hammer of Thor: Norse Mythology and Legends*. El Paso Norte Press, 2010.

Gundarsson, Kveldúlfr and Ben Waggoner, ed. *Things, Signs and Their Meanings: A Dictionary of Heathen Symbols*. New Haven, CT: The Troth, 2010.

Haag, Earl C. *Die Pennsylaanisch Deitsche*. Kutztown, PA: Pennsylvania German Society, 2010.

Heindel, Ned D. *Hexenkopf: History, Healing & Hexerei*. Easton: Northampton County Historical Society Publishers, 2005.

Herr, Karl. *Hex and Spellwork: The Magical Practices of the Pennsylvania Dutch*. York Beach, Maine: Weiser Books, 2002.

Hertzog, Phares H. "Snakelore in Pennsylvania German Folk Medicine." *Pennsylvania Folklife* vol. 17 no. 2, pp. 24-26. Lancaster, PA: Pennsylvania Folklife Society, Winter 1967.

Hess, Susan. *Homestead Herbalism* [course]. Pottstown, PA: Farm at Coventry, 2010.

Hess, Susan. "Mugwort." *Hollerbeier Haven: Newsletter for the Herbal and Healing Arts*, v. 1, no. 3, p. 11. Kempton, PA: Three Sisters Center for the Healing Arts, November 2007.

Hess, Susan. "Nine Sacred Herbs." *Hollerbeier Haven: Newsletter for the Herbal and Healing Arts*, v. 2 no. 1, p. 10. Kempton, PA: Three Sisters Center for the Healing Arts, May 2008.

Hohman, John George. *Pow-Wows or, Long Lost Friend*. Sioux Falls: NuVision Publications, 2007.

Hohman, Johann Georg. *Der Lang Verborgene Freund.* Reading, PA: NP, 1820.

Hollander, Lee M., trans. *Hávámal: Sayings of the High One.* Parksville, BC: Wodanesdag Press, n.d. ISBN: 0-9738423-0-X.

Howells, William. *The Heathens: Primitive Man and His Religion.* Garden City, NY: Doubleday Anchor Books, 1962.

Hyatt, E. Max. *Hávámal: Sayings of the High One.* Parksville, BC: Wodanesdag Press, n.d. ISBN: 0-9738423-0-X.

Jones, Prudence. Pennick, Nigel. *A History of Pagan Europe.* Routledge, 1995. ISBN: 0-415-15804-4

Jordan, Mildred. *The Distelfink Country of the Pennsylvania Dutch.* New York: Crown Publishers, Inc., 1978.

Krasskova, Galina and Raven Kaldera. *Northern Tradition for the Solitary Practitioner.* Franklin Lakes, NJ: New Page Books, 2009.

Kriebel, David W. *Powwowing Among the Pennsylvania Dutch.* University Park: Penn State University Press, 2007.

Lafayllve, Patricia M. *Freyja, Lady, Vanadis.* Denver, CO: Outskirts Press, 2006.

Larrington, Carolyne, trans. *The Poetic Edda.* New York: Oxford University Press, 1996.

Leh, R. R. "Eilaschpiggel... Eisahannes." *The Pennsylvania Dutchman*, vol. 1, no. 7, p. 7. Lancaster, PA: The Pennsylvania Dutch Folklore Center, June 16, 1949.

Lick, David E. "Plant Names and Plant Lore among the Pennsylvania Germans." *Proceedings of the Pennsylvania German Society* 33. Norristown, PA, 1922.

Long, Amos. "Dutch Country Scarecrows." *Pennsylvania Folklife,* vol. 12 no. 3, Fall 1961. Lancaster, PA: The Pennsylvania Folklife Society, pp. 55-59.

Lusch, Robert, 2009. "Living Land." *Hollerbeier Haven: Journal of Traditional Deitsch Wisdom*, p 16. Spring 2009. Kempton, PA: Three Sisters Center.

Marks, David S. "Fretted Dulcimers." *Kutztown Folk Festival* vol. 37, no. 4, pp. 14-17. Kutztown, PA: Pennsylvania Folklife Society, Spring 1988.

Millspaw, Yvonne J. "Witchcraft Belief in a Pennsylvania German Family." *Pennsylvania Folklife* vol. 27, no. 4, pp. 14-24. Lancaster, PA: Pennsylvania Folklife Society, Summer 1978.

Milnes, Gerald C. *Signs, Cures, & Witchery.* Knoxville: University of Tennessee Press, 2007. ISBN: 978-1-57233-577-6.

Montgomery, Jack. *American Shamans: Journeys with Traditional Healers.* Ithaca, NY: Busca, 2009.

Montgomery, Jack. "Traditional Germanic Healing Arts in America: Powwowing." *Hex Magazine*, issue 2, pp. 47-50. Portland, OR: Hex Press, Fall & Winter 2007.

Mutzbauer, Monica. "Leaving the Old World for the New: Rules Governing Emigration from Landau in the Palatinate." *Pennsylvania Folklife* vol. 44 no. 3, pp. 137-144. Collegeville, PA: Pennsylvania Folklife Society, Spring 1995.

Müller-Ebeling, Claudia, Christian Rätsch, and Wolf-Dieter Storl. *Witchcraft Medicine.* Aarau, Switzerland: AT Verlag, 1998.

Nolt, Steven M. *Foreigners in Their Own Land: Pennsylvania Germans in the Early Republic.* University Park: Pennsylvania State University Press, 2002.

Oppenheimer, Paul, trans. *Till Eulenspiegel.* New York: Oxford University Press, 1995.

Padberg, Lutz von. *Bonifatius: Missionar und Reformer.* C.H. Beck, 2003, pp. 41–42. ISBN 9783406480195.

Parsons, William T. *Pennsylvania Germans – A Persistent Minority.* Collegeville, PA: Keschte Bicher, 1976.

Paxson, Diana L. *Essential Asatru.* New York: Citadel, 2006.

Paxson, Diana L. *Taking Up the Runes.* San Francisco: Red Wheel/Weiser LLC, 2005.

Pennick, Nigel. "The Goddess Zisa." *Tyr: Myth, Culture, Tradition* vol. 1, pp. 107-110. Atlanta: Ultra, 2002.

RavenWolf, Silver. *HexCraft: Dutch Country Pow-Wow Magick*. St. Paul: Llewellyn Publications, 1995.

Russell, James C. *The Germanization of Early Medieval Christianity*. New York: Oxford University Press, 1994.

Rüttner-Cova, Sonja. *Frau Holle, die Gestürtzte Göttin: Märchen, Mythen, Matriarchat*. Basel: Sphinx-Verlag, 1993.

Schreiwer, Robert L. *A Brief Introduction to Urglaawe*. Bristol, PA: Deitscherei.com, 2009.

Shaner, Richard H. *Hexerei: A Practice of Witchcraft among the Pennsylvania Dutch*. Indiana, PA: A. G. Halldin, 1963.

Schantz, J.F.J., 1900. *The Domestic Life and Characteristics of the Pennsylvania-German Pioneer*, p 80. Lancaster, PA: The Pennsylvania German Society.

Sheffield, Ann Gróa. *Frey: God of the World*. Raleigh, NC: Lulu.com, 2007.

Sheil, Thor and Audrey Sheil. *Hedenskap: The Folk Religion of Ancient Scandinavia*. Freehold, NJ: Trollwise Press, 1992.

Sheil, Thor and Audrey Sheil. *Old Norse Charms, Spoken Spells and Rhymes*. Freehold, NJ: Trollwise Press, 1992.

Sheil, Thor and Audrey Sheil. *Old Norse Runecraft and Spellcraft*. Freehold, NJ: Trollwise Press, 2007.

Shoemaker, Alfred L. *Eastertide in Pennsylvania*. Mechanicsburg, PA: Stackpole Books, 2000.

Shoemaker, Alfred L. "Belsnickel Lore." *The Dutchman* v. 6 no. 3, Winter 1954-55. Lancaster, PA: The Pennsylvania Dutch Folklore Center.

Shoemaker, Alfred L. "Water Witching." *Pennsylvania Folklife* v. 12 no. 3, Fall 1961. Lancaster, PA: Pennsylvania Folklife Society.

Shoemaker, Alfred L. and Don Yoder. *Christmas in Pennsylvania*. Mechanicsburg, PA: Stackpole Books, 1999.

Sicher, Lauren. "The Tree of Life: Der Lewwebaam." *Hollerbeier Haven* vol. 2 no. 2, pp. 6, 16. Kempton, PA: The Three Sisters Center for the Healing Arts, Fall 2008.

Smith, Norman A. "Der Alt Hexa Zehner." *The Pennsylvania Dutchman*, vol. 1, no. 17, p. 2. Lancaster, PA: The Pennsylvania Dutch Folklore Center, August 25, 1949.

Stine, Eugene S. *Pennsylvania German Dictionary.* Birdsboro, PA: Pennsylvania German Society, 1996.

Stoudt, John B. *The Folklore of the Pennsylvania Germans.* Philadelphia: Pennsylvania German Society, 1916.

Tacitus, Pubilius Cornelius, translated by Herbert W. Benario. "Germany." *Agricola, Germany, and Dialogue on Orators* pp. 63-88. Indianapolis: Hackett Publishing Company, Inc., 2006. ISBN: 0-87220-812-5.

Tatar, Maria, ed. *The Annotated Brothers Grimm.* New York: W. W. Norton, 2004. ISBN: 0-393-05848-4.

Thorsson, Edred. *Futhark: A Handbook of Rune Magic.* San Francisco: Red Wheel/Weiser LLC, 1984.

Tobin, Jesse. *Der Braucherei Weg* [CD; 12-month course]. Kempton, PA: The Three Sisters Center for the Healing Arts, 2008.

Tobin, Jesse. "Es Pennsilfaanisch Muunraad." *Hollerbeier Haven: Newsletter for the Herbal and Healing Arts,* vol. 2 no. 1, p. 4, 8-9. Kempton, PA: Three Sisters Center for the Healing Arts, May 2008.

Tobin, Jesse. "Powwow Birds." *Hollerbeier Haven: Journal of Traditional Deitsch Wisdom,* vol. 1 no. 3, p. 7. Kempton, PA: Three Sisters Center for the Healing Arts, November 2007.

Tobin, Jesse. "Elder Berry Cordial." *Hollerbeier Haven: Journal of Traditional Deitsch Wisdom,* p. 2. Kempton, PA: Three Sisters Center for the Healing Arts, May 2007.

Tobin, Jesse. "May Day!" *Hollerbeier Haven: Journal of Traditional Deitsch Wisdom,* v. 2 no. 1, p. 3. Kempton, PA: Three Sisters Center for the Healing Arts, May 2008.

Tobin, Jesse. "The Praiseworthy Virtues of the North." *Hollerbeier Haven: Newsletter for Herbal and Healing Arts,* v. 1 no. 2, p. 15. Kempton, PA: Three Sisters Center for the Healing Arts, August 2007.

Tobin, Jesse. "The Sacred Promise at Erntedankfescht." *Hollerbeier Haven: Newsletter for Herbal and Healing Arts,* v. 1 no. 2, pp. 14, 16. Kempton, PA: Three Sisters Center for the Healing Arts, August 2007.

Tobin, Jesse. "The Wild Hunt Begins." *Hollerbeier Haven: Journal of Traditional Deitsch Wisdom* v. 1 no. 3, pp. 4, 9, 10, 13, November 2007.

Tobin, Jesse. "Walpurgis Nacht." *Hollerbeier Haven: Newsletter for Herbal and Healing Arts,* v. 1 no. 1, p. 6. Kempton, PA: Three Sisters Center for the Healing Arts, May 2007.

Turville-Petre, Gabriel. *Myth and Religion of the North: The Religion of Ancient Scandinavia.* London: Weidenfeld and Nicolson, 1964.

Von Schönwerth, Franz Xaver, Erika Eichenseer, ed. *Sagen und Märchen aus der Oberpfalz.* Regensburg: E.ON Bayern, 2010.

Weaver, William Woys. *Sauer's Herbal Cures: America's First Book of Botanic Healing.* New York: Routledge, 2001.

Wentz, Richard E. *Pennsylvania Dutch Folk Spirituality.* New York: Paulist Press, 1993.

White, Thomas. *Forgotten Tales of Pennsylvania.* Charleston: The History Press, 2009.

Wieand, Paul R. *Folk Medicine Plants Used in Penna. Dutch Country.* Allentown: Octavo, 1963.

Winey, Fay M. "Belsnickeling in Paxtonville." *Pennsylvania Folklife,* v. 19, no. 2, pp. 10-13. Lancaster, PA: Pennsylvania Folklife Society, Winter 1970.

Winkler, Louis. *Pennsylvania German Astrology and Astronomy.* Lancaster, PA: Pennsylvania Folklife Society, 1982. Note: The content of this book is also present in various articles within *Pennsylvania Folklife* magazine in 1971-1973.

Winkler, Louis. "Pennsylvania German Astrology and Astronomy V: Religion and Astronomy." *Pennsylvania Folklife,* vol. 22, no. 3, pp. 37-40. Lancaster, PA: Pennsylvania Folklife Society, Spring 1973.

Wodening, Eric. *The Heathen Soul*. Columbia, MO: Wednesbury Shire. Retrieved on March 26, 2012 from http://www.englatheod.org/soul.htm.

Wood, Francis Asbury. *The Hildebrandslied*. Chicago: University of Chicago Press, 1914.

Yoder, Don, ed. "A Legend of Alle-Maengel." *The Pennsylvania Dutchman*, vol. 1, no. 12, p. 5. Lancaster, PA: Pennsylvania Dutch Folklore Center, July 21, 1949.

Yoder, Don. *Folk Medicine*. "Folklore and Folklife." University of Chicago Press, 1972.

Yoder, Don. *Groundhog Day*. Mechanicsburg, PA: Stackpole Books, 2003. ISBN: 0-8117-0029-1.

Yoder, Don. "Harvest Home." *Pennsylvania Folklife* v. 9 no. 4, pp. 2-11. Lancaster, PA:The Pennsylvania Folklife Society, Fall 1958.

Yoder, Don. "Hex Signs and Magical Protection of House and Barn: Folk-Cultural Questionnaire No. 35." *Pennsylvania Folklife* vol. 22 Folk Festival Supplement, inside cover. Lancaster, PA: Pennsylvania Folklife Society, 1974.

Yoder, Don. "Trance-Preaching in the United States." *Pennsylvania Folklife* vol. 18 no. 2, pp. 12-18. Lancaster, PA: The Pennsylvania Folklife Society, Winter 1968.

Yoder, Don. "Twenty Questions on Powwowing." *Pennsylvania Folklife* vol. 15, no. 4, pp. 38-40. Lancaster, PA: Pennsylvania Folklife Society, Summer 1966.

Yoder, Don. "The Strouse Dance." *Pennsylvania Folklife* vol. 9 no. 1, pp. 12-17. Lancaster, PA: Pennsylvania Dutch Folklore Center, Winter 1958.

Yoder, Don and Thomas E. Graves. *Hex Signs*. Mechanicsburg, PA: Stackpole Books, 2000.

BCTV Pennsylvania German: Interview with Patrick Donmoyer (http://www.bctv.org/WatchArchive.aspx?id=1552)

Appendix I - Pronunciation of Pennsylvania German (Deitsch)

Vowels	Sample Deitsch Word	English Approximation
a (short)	Sache	a as in what
aa (long)	Aag, Urglaawe	aw as in saw
ae (long)	Baer	ea as in bear
ae (short)	Paesching	a as in match
ar (long)	darf	a as in father
e (long)	geht, weech	a as in gate
e (short)	fett	e as in get
i (long)	ihn, Iewing	ee as in see
i (short)	bin	i as in pin
o (long)	rot, Boot	oa as in boat
o (short)	Kopp	u as in cup
u (long)	Blut, Bu	oo as in moon
u (short)	dumm	oo as in cook

Diphthongs	Sample Deitsch Word	English Approximation
au	laut	ow as in cow
ei	Greisch	i as in pine
oi	Roi	oy as in boy

Consonants	Sample Deitsch Word	English Approximation
b	Bank	b as in bank
ch	Ich	sound not in English. Similar to a dramatic h as in huge
ch	acht	sound not in English. Similar to the above but deeper in throat.
ck	Pack	as in English back
d	Dodder	similar to English d except at end of word, where it often sounds like a t
f	finne	similar to English f
g	Geld	g as in gold
g (between two vowels)	Aage	sound not in English. Falls between a g and a y
g (final position)	Aag	k as in kick
gg	Reggeboge	sound not in English. Falls between a g and a y
h	Hut	as in English hat
h (silent)	Uhr	merely prolongs the vowel
l	Leicht	similar to English l
m	Mann	similar to English m
n	Not	similar to English n
ng	Ring	as in singer, never finger
nk	genunk	similar to English nk

Consonants	Sample Deitsch Word	English Approximation
p	Paar	similar to English p
r	Raahm, Urglaawe	trilled or (rarely) uvular in initial; trilled in medial; vocal after vowel before consonant, or at end of word. If vocalic r is intervocalic, use consonantal r sound
s	Saddel, Sege	similar to English s
sch	Schul	sh as in shop
t	Tee	similar to English t
v	verrickt	as in English f
w	Wasser	as in English v, some areas as in English w
x	Hex	as in English x
x	waxe	sometimes as though saying Deitsch ch-s
y	yung	y as in yard
z	Zucker	ts as in hats

Portions of the table above were drawn from Eugene S. Stine's *Pennsylvania German Dictionary.*

INDEX

A

Aadler, 3
Aarufing, 3
Abbel, 3, 72
Abbelseider, 14
aconite, 74
Addning, 3, 50
Ael, 3, 14
Aernet, 3
Aesir, 4, 53, 74
Alcis, 3, 4
Aldaar, 3
Aldi Fraa, 4
álfar, 19
Alhiz, 3
Alleliaweziel, 5, 10, 11, 14, 24, 54, 56, 59
Allemaengel, 5, 34
All-Father, 68
Alsatian, 74
Alt Fraa. See Aldi Fraa
alu, 5
amber, 26
American Goldfinch, 13
Amish, 12, 27, 39, 45
amulet, 6, 9
ancestors, 17, 19, 41, 44, 47, 54, 71
ancillary virtue, 5, 15, 25, 30, 46, 48, 51, 59, 63, 64, 66
Angelica Lake, 36
Anglo-Saxon, 4, 11, 49, 52, 69
Ansuz, 5
Appalachia, Appalachian, 10, 54
Apple, 3
apple cider, 14, 59

April, 49
April Fool, 68
Arminius, 60
Ásatrú, 29, 53
Ase, 5, 43, 64
Aseheem, 43
Asgard, 43
Augsburg, 72, 73
August, 3, 39
Ausdauer, 5, 50
Ausdeeling, 5
Austria, 68

B

badger, 32
Baer, 5, 28
Balder, 6, 27, 50
Baltimore, 12
Bann, 6
Banner, 6
Bannerei, 7
Banning charm, 6
Banshee, 65
Barick, 7
barn star, 37, 39
Barricke Mariche, 47
Barrickschpitz, 6
Barrow, 6, 30, 42
Battle of Teutoburg Forest, 60
Bavaria, 72
Bear, 5
Bedenk, 7
Bedrachdung, 7
beer, 14
Beifuß, 4

Belsnickel, 7, 68, 69
Belsnickeling, 48, 68, 71
Berchta, Berchtaslaafe 4, 8, 17, 29, 55, 66, 70
Berkano, 27
Berks County, 5, 36, 50
Beyfuss, 4
Bier, 14
Birch, 27, 50
Bird of Paradise, 14
Blanzeschwetze, 8, 11
Blobarrick, 6, 20, 41
Blobottel, 8
Bloodletting, 9
Blue Mountain, 6, 20-21, 36
Blutvergiesse, 9, 22, 59
bowl, 3, 54
Braucher, 9, 35, 67
Braucherei, 7, 9, 11, 16, 21, 25, 29, 32, 34, 35, 36, 40, 42, 43, 45, 47, 48, 49, 52, 53, 55, 60, 68, 70, 71, 74
Braucherin, 9
breath of life, 10, 49, 57, 68
Brechtelweheem, 19, 44
Brechthelft, 10, 40, 56
Brides, 39
Bright Half, 10, 40, 56
Brocken, 35, 40
Broochet, 10
Brunn, 10
Bschluss, 10
Buckliches Männli, Buckliches Mennli, 10
butchering season, 54
Butz, 10, 11
Butzemann, 10, 11, 24, 32, 56

C

Carbon County, 37, 68
Castor and Pollux, 4
catnip, 49
Cats, 26, 37
caul, 20
Centaurea cyanus, 8
Centre County, PA, 37

ceremonial grounds, 34, 39
chaos, 29
Charm ticket, 71
charms, 6, 9, 34, 45, 50, 64
chickens, 24, 37
cinquefoil, 49
cleansing, 11, 51
Clergy, 13
Colors, 22, 52
Compassion, compassionate, 25, 40, 46, 51
Computus, 23
conjurations, 9
consciousness, 5, 14, 25, 29, 48, 59, 60
consumer culture, 63, 64
cornflower, Cornflower Queen, 8
cosmic, 19, 23, 33, 72
Courage, 44, 46
courtyard, 39
creative life force, 69
Croatia, 23
Crow, 31
Curiosity, 48, 51
Cushion Peak, 6, 30
Custom, 20, 29, 32, 90

D

Daaf, 11, 63
daafe, 11
dark force, 36
Dark Half, 14, 56, 66, 67
death, 10, 20, 22, 25, 27-28, 29, 40, 44, 51, 53, 56, 57, 65, 69
deities, 3, 4, 5, 14, 17, 22, 28, 29, 31, 34, 38, 43, 45, 51, 54, 59, 65, 66, 69, 70, 72
Deitsch, 12
Deitschdaag, 12
Deitscherei, 6, 12, 13, 15, 23, 24, 33, 35, 36, 40, 48, 54, 55, 60, 68, 71
Delaware, Delaware River, 12
der Mechdich Eech, 25
descendants, 11, 71
Deutsch, 12

Die Nein Welte, 43
Diener, Dienerin, 13
Dienstag, 74
Ding, 16, 33, 39, 65
Dinschdaag, 65
Discipline, 3, 50, 60, 63, 74
disposition, 30, 48, 58
distaff, 27, 34, 65
Distelfink, 13, 14, 52
Distribution, 6
Divination, 64
divine, 30, 53, 65
Divinity, 23, 44
dogwood, 49
Doom of the Gods, 29
Drankopfer, 14
Dreizehdax, 51
Drinkhann, 14, 59
Drinking horn, 6, 14, 59
dulcimer, 54
dumpling, 8
Dunkelgegend, 44
Dunkelhelft, 14, 56, 67
Dunner, 14, 15, 16, 21, 34, 38
Dunnerhammer, 15, 33, 41
Dunnerkeil, 15, 53
Dunnerschdaag, 15
Duty, 45, 49, 63, 64
Dwarf, 75
Dwayyo, 55

E

Eagle, 3, 13
Eagle's Peak, 15, 36
Earth-mirror, 20
East Leaves, 44
Edelmut, 15, 25, 51, 64
Edelreenheide, 16, 50
Eech, 15, 16
Eed, 16
Eedring, 17
Ehr, 17, 50
ehre, 17
Eil, 17, 66
Eilaading, 18
Eileschpiggel, Til, 17

Eir, 66
Eisehannes, 18
Elbdraam, 19
Elbedritsch, 18, 48
Elbekeenich, 18, 19, 65
elder, elderberry, 29, 39, 41, 49
Elf-king, 18
Elfschuss, 20
Elf-shot, 20
Elhaz, 4
Elk Creek Gap, 37
Elweheim, 19, 44
emotions, 23, 31
England, 68
entrance (put into a trance), 30
Entzicke, 20, 26
Erdgeischt, 20, 75
Erdschpiggel, 20
Erlkeenich, 18
Erlking, 18
Erlkönig, 18
Erntfescht, 10, 20, 46, 56
Es Bucklich Männli, 10
Eternal Hunter, 5, 18, 20, 21-22, 36, 41, 61, 66
ethic, 7, 15, 74
European Goldfinch, 13
Ewicher Yeeger, 5, 18, 20, 21-22, 36, 41, 61, 66

F

Faas, 24
Fagge, 22, 59
Fain, 22, 59
fairy godmothers, 41
Farewe, 22
Fasching, 23, 24, 68
Fastnachts, 23
feast, 54
Feast of Frey, 70
February, 23, 27, 33
Feierheim, 44
Fenris, 34
Fetch, 25, 57, 58
Fidelity, 50, 61
Fimf-Fingergraut, 49

fire, 24, 29, 30, 44, 53, 60
fish, 8, 36
folk doctor, 9
Folyer, 25, 58
Forn Sidu, vii
Forrell, 25, 48
Frankish, 41
Frau-Holle-Teich, 40
Freibesitz, 26, 65
Freindschaft, 26, 47, 48, 50, 53, 64
Frey, 26, 61, 66, 70
Freya, 26, 65, 66
Friday, 15, 38
Frigg, 5, 6, 11, 27, 33, 38, 45, 50, 55, 64, 65, 70
Frog, 27
Frosch, 27
Frost Giants, 51
Fruchsfriede, 27, 28, 49
Fuffzehfux, 51
Fulla, 50, 64
funerary procession, 42
Furious Host, 67
Fux, 6, 28
Fylfot, 39

G

Gans, 8, 28, 41
Garyel, 14, 29
Gathering, 53
Gebo, 43
Gebrauch, 29
Gedderdemmerung, 29, 72
Gedechnisleicht, 29
Gedechniszettel, 29, 42
Gefjon, 5, 48
Gegende, 52
Gehling, 5, 12, 14, 30
Geischt, 30, 57
Geischtlichkeet, 30, 51
Gemiet, 30, 52
Gemietlichkeet, 28, 30, 31
Generosity, 15, 25, 51
German, 12
German Heathenry, 38
Germantown, 12

Germany, 8, 9, 35, 41, 68, 72
Getz, 31
Gewut, 31, 58
Gewwern, 52
Ghost, 30, 55, 57
Giants, 43, 51, 52
gift, 15, 16, 28, 32, 33, 46, 54, 56, 59, 61, 64, 67, 69
Gift (poison), 72
Glick, 31, 57, 58
glove, 34, 65, 74
Glove Rite, 34
gloves, 65
gnomes, 19, 20, 75
Gnostic, 33
goats, 14, 15
god, goddess, 3, 4, 8, 14, 21, 26, 29, 32, 33, 36, 40, 41, 43, 45, 49, 50, 51, 52, 55, 60, 61, 62, 64, 66, 72, 74
godsman, godswoman, 4, 72
goose, 4, 28, 29, 64
Grabb, 31, 48
ground ivy, 49
Groundhog, 6, 13, 28, 31, 32
Groundhog Day, 23, 24, 32
grove, 17, 34
gruel, 8
Grundsau, 6, 28, 31, 32, 48
Grundsaudaag, 10, 23, 42, 56
Gschenk, 32
guardian angels, 41
guideline, 52
guiding principle, 8, 52
Guild, 26, 47, 48, 50

H

Hadding, 14, 26, 33
Hadubrand, 27-28
Haerdziebin, 33
Hagalaz, 52
Halloween, See *Allelieweziel*
hallowing, 33, 34, 38
Hamburg, PA, 67
Hammer, 15, 33, 65
Hammer and Sickle Rite, 33

Hammer Rite, 33
Hammerbrauch, 15, 33
Hammer-un-Sichel Brauch, 33
Hanning, 27, 33
harvest, 20, 39
Harvest Home, 20
Hatzholz, 44
Hauslauch, 15, 34
Haussege, 34, 71
Hávamál, 32, 62
Hawk Mountain, 6
haymaking, 39
healer, 9, 35
hearth, 11, 27, 32, 33, 56
Hearth Goddess, 33
Heathen, 8, 9, 11, 13, 14, 15, 16, 17, 18, 21, 23, 25, 27, 32, 34, 37, 38, 39, 41, 42, 43, 45, 47, 50, 54, 55, 57, 59, 60, 62, 63, 64, 66, 68, 69, 70, 74
Heathenism, 34
Heathenry, 11, 14, 15, 16, 18, 34, 38, 41, 48, 50, 54, 60, 62, 63, 69
Heid, Heidn 34
Heidetum, 34
Heidin, 33
heidisch, 34
heiliche, 34
Heiliching, 34
Hein, 34, 39
Helheem, 44
Helm of Awe, 16
hematite, 35
Hengist, 4
Henschingbrauch, 34
herbal teas, 14
herbs, 4, 49
heritage, 42
herring, 8
Hessia, Hessian 12, 40, 74
Hex, 34
hex sign, 16, 22, 34, 37, 39, 43, 52, 53
Hexebaerrick, 34, 35
Hexedanz, 34
Hexefeld, 35

Hexekopp, 34, 35
Hexekoppwasser, 35
Hexemeeschder, 35
Hexenkopf, 6, 35, 40, 41
Hexerei, 7, 16, 34, 35, 36, 68, 71
Hexeschild. See *Hexezeeche*
Hexewolf, 36, 37, 55
Hexezeeche, 37, 52
Higher Self, 38, 58, 67
Hildebrand, 27-28
Hildebrandslied, 27-28
Himmelgegend, 43-44
Hoch, 38, 57, 58
Hochzich, 38
Hof, 39
Hohegegend, 44
Hoherer Selbscht, 67
Hoiet, 39
Hoietfescht, 26, 39, 56
Hokekreiz, 39-40
Holle, 4, 5, 8, 10, 11, 14, 21, 25, 26, 28, 29, 33, 35, 40-41, 45, 46, 52, 53, 55, 60, 65, 66
Hollebeer, 41
Holler, 41
Hollesichel, 33, 41
Holzent, 41, 48
Holzhaahne, 41, 48
Honor, 17, 50
Hoodoo, 10
horehound, 49
Horsa, 4
Hospitality, 15, 50, 62, 63
Hottenstein, 41, 52
House blessing, 34
houseleek, 14, 34

I

Icelandic, 16
Idis, 41, 44
idol, 31
Idunn, 3, 5, 72
Illinois, 12
imp, 10
incantations, 6, 7, 9, 33, 35, 45, 50, 60, 64, 71

incense, 3, 4
Indiana, 12
Industriousness, 50, 53
Ing, 61
Ingvaeones, 61
Ingwaz, 52, 53
intent, 68
Introspection, 14, 51, 59
Invitation, 18
Invocation, 3, 31
Irminen, 62
Irminones, 61
Irminsul, 41-42
Iron John, 18
Istvaeones, 61
Iwwerliefering, 42

J

January, 14, 26, 33, 70, 76
Jera, 40, 53
Jersey Devils, 36
Jim Thorpe, 37
Jotunheim, 43
journeywork, 18, 25, 26, 57
July, 39
June, 10, 31

K

Kenaz, 53
King Frost, 51, 67
Kinship, 27, 51, 64
Kittatinny Ridge, 21
Knecht Rubrecht, 70
Krefeld, 12

L

Lacnunga, 49
Laguz, 14, 52
Lancaster County, 35, 36
Landauer, Landauerin, 42
legacy, 26, 42
Leich, 42, 58
Leicht, 42, 57
Leichtfeier, 7, 42

Leichtlaaf, 42
Lenape, 9, 36
Lenzbutzerei, 42
Lenzing, 42
Lewesbaam, 19, 31, 41, 42, 44, 48
Lewesraad, 44, 57
Leweszeeche, 45
libation, 5, 6, 14, 22, 29, 54, 59
life, 3, 8, 10, 11, 23, 25, 28, 29, 31, 37, 40, 41, 42, 43, 44, 47, 48, 49, 53, 56, 58, 62, 63, 68, 69, 74, 75
life force, 60, 69
Light Half, See *Bright Half*
lightning, 14, 34
lineage, 26, 27
Luck, 11, 14, 31, 36, 58

M

magician, 6, 71
Mannheem, 34, 43
Mannus, 61
March, 42
Mardi Gras, 23, 68
Maryland, 12, 55
Matres and Matrones, 70
Mauch Chunk, 37
May, 49, 51, 66, 69
Maypole, 50, 69
mead, 14, 45
Meditation, 7
Megge, 45, 58, 60
Meind, 45, 58
Mennonites, 12
Menschepflicht, 45
Merseburg Incantations, 45, 50, 64
Mesopust, 23-24
Met, 14, 45
Metzelsupp, 54
Midgard, 43
Midsummer, 31, 45, 56, 62
Miehl, 5, 41, 46
Mighty Oak, 16
Migration, 8, 9
Mill, 46, 53
Mimir's Well, 10

mind, 23, 37, 45, 61
Mitleid, 25, 40, 46, 51
Mjölnir, 15, 53
Moifescht, 10, 34, 47, 56, 59
Mood, 30, 58
Moon Wheel, 48
Moral duty, 45
Moravians, 12
Mother Goose, 28
Mother Night, 47
Mount Penn, 6, 36
Mount Pisgah, 6
mountain ash, 15
Mountain Mary, 47, 50
Muddernacht, 47
mugwort, 4
Multiverse, 29
Mummer's Parade, 47, 68
Mumming, 47
Muspelheem, 44
Mut, 48, 50
Muunraad, 2, 3, 6, 17, 18, 25, 27, 28, 31, 41, 48, 54, 55, 64

N

Nadd, 26, 40, 66
Naddbledder, 44
Naharnavali, 4
Naudhiz, 52
Nazis, 39
Neigierheit, 48, 51
Neiyaahrsdaag, 56
Nerthus, 40
Netherlands Dutch, 70
New Year's blessings, 47
New Year's Day, 17, 64
New Year's Resolution, 16-17, 56, 59
New York, 12
Newwelheem, 44
Newweling, 49, 51
Newwereenheide, 48, 51
nightmare, 19
Nine Noble Virtues, 15, 16, 50-51
Nine Regions Cosmology, 44
Nine Sacred Herbs, 49

Nine Worlds Cosmology, 43
Njörðr, 26, 40, 66
Noble Virtue, 15, 16, 50-51
Nodd, 26, 40
Norns, 45, 55, 69-70
North Carolina, 12
North Leaves, 44
North Star, 74
Northampton County, 35
November, 49, 50, 51, 67

O

Oak, 15, 16
Oath, 16, 17, 26, 49, 53, 56, 60, 64
oath ring, 17
oatmeal, 8
Ochdem, 10, 49, 57
October, 5, 12, 14, 30, 40, 67
Odem, 10, 49, 57
Odin, 10, 62, 65, 68
Offering, 3, 10, 22, 28, 49, 54
Ohio, 12
Oley, 36, 47, 50, 64
Ontario, 12
Opfer, 49
Order, 49, 62
Ordning, 49, 62
Ørlög, 62
Oschdra, 49
Oschdraslaaf, 49
Oschdre, 49, 56
Oschdret, 49
Oschtbledder, 44
owl, 17, 66

P

Pagoda, 36
Painted Bunting, 13
Palatinate, 42, 74
Palatine, 5, 12
peace, 22, 27, 28, 29
Pennsylvania Dutch, See *Deitsch*
Pennsylvania German, See *Deitsch*
Pennsylvania German Cultural Heritage Center, 16, 33

Perseverance, 5, 50
Pflicht, 49
Philadelphia, 8, 12, 47, 68
Phol, 27, 50, 64
Pike Township, 50
Pilgrimage, 50
Pilyerrees, 50
Pine Barrens, 36
pinecone, 73
Pinnacle, 6, 36
Powwow, powwowing, 9, 66
protection, 11, 22, 34, 38
Prussia, 8
Puck, 10, 11
puppy mills, 75
Puritans, 70
Purpose, 75
pyre, 7, 29, 42

Q

Queschtbaam, 50, 69

R

Raad, 50
Raane, 52
Ragnarök, 29
Raidho, 53
Reamstown, 35
rebirth, 10, 23, 25, 29, 40, 44, 46, 53, 56, 65
red, 15, 39, 53, 70
Reenheide, 3, 6, 15, 16, 17, 25, 30, 46, 48, 49, 50, 51, 53, 59, 61, 62, 63, 64, 66
Regel, 51
Reifkeenich, 51, 67
Reifries, 14, 51, 52
reindeer, 70
Reiniching, 51
rheumatism, 15
Richtschnur, 52
riddles, 69
Ries, 43, 51, 52
Rieseheem, 43
rob, 14, 29

Roon, 7, 40, 52, 64
Roonfaahne, 52
rowan, 15
Ruckschtee, 15, 53
rule, 51
Rune, 4, 6, 7, 23, 27, 40, 51, 52, 53, 57, 58, 59, 64, 68, 74
Rune banners, 52
Rune Gild, 57-58

S

Sacred Duty, 63, 74
Sacred Promise, 56, 74, 75
sacrifice, 9, 10, 11, 27, 34
sage, 49
Saint Nicholas, 68, 69, 70
Sammel, 16, 53, 54
Santa Claus, 68, 70
Scandinavian, 3, 5, 10, 14, 15, 19, 26, 27, 34, 41, 43, 50, 52, 60, 62, 64, 65, 66, 69, 75
scarecrow, 10, 11
Schaffichheit, 50, 53
Scheiding, 53, 74
Scheierschtann, 37, 39, 54
Scheitholt, 54
Schillgrott, 48, 54
Schissel, 3, 6, 54
Schlachtzeit, 5, 32, 54
Schmaus, 54
Schneller Geischt, 55
Schpeecht, 48, 55
Schpindelbrauch, 27, 55
Schpuck, 55
Schtaab, 60
Schtarich, 55
Schwatzelweheem, 43
Schwatzer Piet, 70
Schwerpunkt, 55
scruple, 7, 52
Seasonal Focus, 55
security, 28, 64
Seeker, 48, 68, 69
Seel, 31, 38, 42, 45, 56, 57, 62, 68
Seelhaut, 57, 59

Sege, 6, 9, 11, 16, 22, 54, 59, 62, 75
Segezweig, 6, 54, 59, 76
Seidel, 3, 5, 6, 14, 59
Seider, 14, 59
Selbschtreiguck, 51, 59
Selbschtverbessering, 51, 59
Selbschtzuverdraue, 50, 59, 64
Self, 17, 25, 38, 57, 58, 67
Self-Improvement, 51, 59
Self-Reliance, 50, 59, 64
September, 53, 60, 74
Sessrumnir, 65
shaman, 9, 20, 26
shamanism, 27
Shield Maidens, 65
Shrove Tuesday, 23-24
shrubs, 49
Sichelbrauch, 55, 60
Sickle, 34, 41, 60, 65
Sickle Rite, 60
Silesia, Silesian 4, 12, 74
Sippschaft, 13, 28, 31, 39, 60, 62, 65
Siwwa, 5
Skuld, 70
Sky God, 74
Snallygaster, 55
snow, snowfall, 29, 35, 40
solstice, 45, 47, 56, 62. See *Midsummer, Yuul*
Sophia, 33
sorcerer, sorceress 20, 34, 35
soul, 5, 11, 14, 22, 23, 25, 29, 30, 31, 40, 42, 45, 46, 53, 55, 56, 57-58, 62, 65, 67, 68
soul hunters, 65
South Leaves, 54
Sowilo, 52
spears, 74
Spessart Forest, 41
spindle, 27, 65
Spindle Rite, 55
spirit, 10, 20, 23, 25, 27, 30, 40, 41, 58
Spirituality, 22, 30, 32, 48, 51, 53

spook, 55
Spring Cleaning, 32, 42, 56, 66
Spring Equinox, See *Oschdre*
sprinkling water, 6, 11, 59
statuary, 3, 31, 34
Stav, 60
Steadfastness, 5, 6, 22, 50
Steuben Parade, 8
Stewardship, 51, 63, 74
stork, 55
Straussdanz, 60
Strouse Dance, 60
Suddbledder, 44
Suevi, 72-73
sumble, 53
summer solstice, 45
Sunna, 45, 47, 62
Swabian, Swabians, 12, 47, 72, 74
swastika, 39-40
Swedish, 68
Swirling Swastika, 39-40
Swiss, Swiss German, 12, 74
Switzerland, 8, 72

T

talisman, 15, 71
tea, 51-52
Teitonisch, 60
Teutoburgschlacht, 60
Teutonic, 8, 10, 14, 27, 43, 45, 60, 70
thanksgiving, 20
The Erlking, 18
The Pinnacle, 6, 36
Theodish, 53, 57
thew, 7, 45, 49, 51, 52, 62, 65
Thing, 13
Thistle Finch, 13-14
Thor, 14, 15, 21
Thor's Hammer, 15, 41
Three Sisters, 69
Thrym's Poem, 64
thunder, 14, 15, 21, 22
thunderbolt, 15
Thursday, 15, 38
thyme, 49

time-cord, 20, 46, 71-72
Titus Annius, 72
Tiw, 74
Tiwaz, 74
tower lantern, 62
Tradition, 42
trance, 20, 26
Tree of Life, 41, 42, 43, 44
Treie, 50, 61
trickster, 17, 18, 22
Troth, 50, 61
Truth, 18, 48, 50, 65
Tuesday, 15, 23, 24, 38, 47
Tuisto, 21, 42, 61, 66
Turmlutzer, 62
Turtle, 54
Twelfth Night, 70, 76
twig, 6, 51, 54, 59, 76
Tyr, 13, 34, 42, 72, 74
Tyr's Helm, 74

U

Ufffassing, 49, 62
Uffwaarting, 50, 62
umbilical cords, 71
Undoer-of-Knots, 73
Universe, 29, 45, 48, 56
Unnergegend, 44
Urboge, 62
Urðr, 70
Urglaawer, Urglaawern, 8, 32, 38, 42, 47, 57, 61, 62, 65, 67, 69
Urleeg, 25, 57, 58, 59, 62, 69, 70, 73
Uruz, 5, 23, 52

V

Valhalla, 65
Valkyrie, 65
values, 52, 61, 65
Vanaheim, 43
Vanir, 26, 43, 66
Vatni Ausa, 11
Vatzehvedder, 51
Verðandi,, 70

Verwalting, 45, 51, 63, 74
Verwandschaft, 51, 64
vines, 49
Virgin Mary, 73
Virginia, 12, 71, 77
Virginville, 34
Voll, 5, 27, 50, 64
Volla, 5, 27, 50, 64
Vorsatz, 10, 59, 64

W

Waahr, 38, 64
Waahra, 64
Waahretsaagerei, 64
Waahrheit, 50, 65
Waertunge, 65
Walburga, 66
Walkyrie, 41, 65
Walpurgisnacht, 5, 14, 31, 34, 35, 40, 42, 56, 66, 68, 69
Wanderer, 69
Wane, 5, 8, 21, 26, 40, 43, 61, 65, 66
Waneheem, 43
War of 1812, 12
Wasser, 14, 35, 66
Wassernix, 66
Wasserschpritz. See *Daaf*
water, 10, 11, 14, 27, 35, 67
wedding, 15, 37, 38, 39
Wednesbury Shire, 57-58
Weisheit, 5, 51, 66
Weisskeppichi Fraa, 66, 67
Well, 10, 46
Welsh Mountains, 36
weregild, 28
Weschtbledder, 44
West Leaves, 44
West Virginia, 12, 71
Westphalian, 74
Wheel, 50
whirlwinds, 40
White Marsh Theod, 57, 59
White-Haired Woman, 66
Wicht, 19, 49, 67
Widdergeburt, 65, 67

wight, 3, 11, 17, 19, 20, 28, 36, 49, 66, 67
Wild Hunt, 5, 8, 11, 14, 21, 35, 40, 47, 54, 57, 59, 66, 67,-68, 69, 70, 71
Wild Man, 18
Will, 58, 68
Wille, 58, 68
Winsch, 68
Winter Solstice, See *Yuul*
wintergreen, 49
Wisconsin, 12
Wisdom, 5, 8, 10, 17, 33, 51, 66, 69
Wish-Granter, 68
witch, 4, 17, 34, 35, 37, 69
witch doctor, 9
Witch's Head, 35
Witches Dances. See *Witches Dance*
Witches' Dance, 34, 60
Witches' Field, 35
Witches' Hill, 34
Wodan, 5, 6, 7, 10, 21, 27, 40, 45, 49, 62, 68, 69, 70, 71
wolves, 37
Wonnet, 49, 51, 66, 69
Wonnetdanz, 10, 34, 47, 50, 56, 69
wood duck, 25, 41
woodcock, 41
woodpecker, 55
worship, 4, 17, 61
Wotan, 68
wreath, 17
Wudan, 5, 6, 7, 10, 21, 27, 40, 45, 49, 62, 68, 69, 70, 71
Wurt, 25, 26, 27, 62, 69, 75
Wurthexe, 45, 55, 70
Wyomissing Creek, 67
Wyrd, 45, 62, 69, 74

Y

yellow, 22, 23, 53
Yellow Mountain, 6
Ymir, 61
Yorinde un Goringel, 8, 17
Yuletide, 29, 47
Yuul, 48, 54, 56, 59, 62, 68, 70
Yuuling, 8, 71
Yuulzeit, 47

Z

Zauber, 71
Zauberei, 34, 35, 71, 72
Zauberer, Zaubererin, 71
Zauberzettel, 71
Zeitschnur, 71
Zeitschnurwaerrick, 25, 71
Zieb, Ziebin, Ziewe, 17, 30, 72
Ziewer, Ziewerin, 13, 72
Zing, 6, 72
Zisa, 5, 72, 73, 74
Zisasege, 74
Zistag, 73
zither, 54
Ziu, 5, 13, 15, 34, 38, 39, 42, 61, 65, 72, 73, 74
Zizarim, 72-73
Zusaagfassing, 74
Zusaagpflicht, 8, 45, 56, 63, 74, 75
Zwarich, 75
Zwarichheim, 43
Zweck, 75
Zweig. 76 See *Segezweig*
Zwelfdi Nacht, 76

Þ

Þrymskviða, 64

Made in the USA
Coppell, TX
31 January 2022